TYPES
of
PEOPLE

How to Counsel Them Biblically

JAY E. ADAMS

TIMELESS TE)
STANLEY, N

Contents

Index

Initial Matters

Those who come for counseling are either believers or unbelievers. Your first task is to do your best in making an informed judgment about this. Of course, if they are members of your congregation presumably (unless your policies are less than biblical) you would have been reasonably sure that they are believers before you baptized them or received them into membership. The fact is, however, as your counseling becomes known, you will find that an appreciable number of unbelievers also will come for counseling. So, you should know what to do to discover whether or not you will need to pre-counsel a would-be counselee.

By pre-counseling (as the word indicates) I mean evangelizing unbelievers. It is important not to knowingly counsel an unbeliever. There are a number of reasons for this. I shall mention but two:

1. Unbelievers cannot change in ways that please God. This is clear from Romans 8:8: "Those who are in the flesh can't please God." The unbeliever is incapable of doing whatever is necessary to do to satisfy God's commands. He now pursues a lifestyle that is displeasing to God. Were you to counsel him, the best you could do for him is to help him change his lifestyle to one that may better please him, but would still displease God. That would be unprofitable to Him.

2. And, it would be deceptive. Since this unbeliever is engaged in *biblical* counseling, he should expect to receive Christian counsel. But if he goes away, pleased with what takes place (even though it did not please God), thinking that he has received God's counsel, you will have deceived him. In doing so, you will have placed him in greater jeopardy than before he came. Now he may wrongly conceive of his new lifestyle as one that is truly biblical when,

at best, it only outwardly conforms to God's standards. We have enough Pharisees; it surely isn't the task of biblical counselors to make more!

So, it is important to determine, as best you can, whether you must pre-counsel before attempting to counsel a counselee. Certainly, you must realize, it is (to say the least) unprofitable to help a counselee exchange one lifestyle that leads to eternal damnation for another that does the same.

You will not always be able to determine whether a counselee is or is not a believer. That is because God has reserved the prerogative of reading hearts for Himself. He alone is the "Heart-Knower" (Acts 1:24). Moreover, in II Chronicles 6:30, we read, "You [God], alone know the human heart." The same fact is reiterated several times in Scripture. We read for instance, that "man looks on the outward appearance, but God looks on the heart" (I Samuel 16:7). Since it is the "outer" man with which you will be dealing how, then, will you know? Two factors will enable you to make a reasonable, but always possibly fallible, judgment: 1) consider what one says about himself and 2) what he does – that is, by his words and his ways.

One way of deciding about the issue is to read what the counselee has written on his P.D.I.[1] Among the several questions asked, there is one that inquires about whether the person is "saved." He is given the three options of answering "Yes," "No," and "Not sure what you mean." A solid "No," response greatly helps you. Almost assuredly, you will need to precounsel such a person. The other two responses will not so readily help. They will require further questioning by you. Probing deeper is essential whenever the answer is "Not sure what you mean." Most likely, the person answering in that way will not be a Christian, but, upon further investigation,

---

1. The Personal Data Inventory (PDI) is used by many Nouthetic counselors. On it are questions that are intended to help counselors determine the matter. A copy of the PDI may be found in the Appendix, and may be reproduced on 8 1/2" x 11" paper.

may turn out to be one after all. Though unusual, he may not be used to such language. When a person says, "Yes," if he attends what to your knowledge is a sound church, you should accept this response as true unless later facts prove otherwise. After all, it is fundamentally the responsibility of the church, not individuals, to determine the matter. If his congregation is questionable, it may be necessary to make further inquiries.

How might one do so? To the response "I'm not sure," you will want to determine whether it is a lack of saving faith or whether it is a lack of assurance on the part of a genuine Christian. Each of these determinations should lead you to respond differently. If you determine that the uncertainty stems from the former, you will want to proceed immediately to pre-counseling. If from the latter, you will want to determine what, in particular, is behind his lack of assurance. There are several possibilities, of which the following two are the chief: a.) *flawed teaching* (which most frequently will have to do with the erroneous idea that once saved, a person may again be lost); b.) *unconfessed sin* that makes the counselee wonder about his salvation ("Could I really be a Christian and do...?"). In each case you will want to proceed differently according to the parameters of the situation.

What I have considered in this chapter is initial matters, as the title of the chapter makes clear. We turn now to specific attitudes and actions that you will discover in counselees who qualify for counseling because they are, so far as you can tell, genuine believers.

Anxious to Cooperate

These are persons that you will look forward to counseling; that is, so long as they are well-informed about Nouthetic Counseling and truly want to please God. That is a winning combination! For the most part, they make counseling easy. You will find little resistance. So there is not much sense discoursing about them. It is those Christians who are anxious to receive help, but who *will* create problems for you, even though they truly desire help, that it is necessary to consider. Such persons may, at the outset seem quite anxious to cooperate until something arises (possibly, a homework assignment[1] that displeases them) about which they disapprove, or that they find unpleasant.

There are, moreover, those who claim to be familiar with Nouthetic Counseling but actually, as you will soon discover, know little or nothing of the sort, or have distorted views concerning it. You will often find that people like these may pose a serious problem when you seek their cooperation. This is true, especially, when their motive for coming is other than a desire to please God – which is usually the case.

One reason Christians come for counsel is because they have been encouraged by others who have been helped or who know someone who has. Another reason for their initial enthusiasm is that they hope to find relief from some problem. This, perhaps, is the most frequently encountered motive of all. Unless you can convince such counselees that this goal must not dominate their concerns, it will pose a threat to the

---

1. This is no place to discuss homework, which is considered in depth in *The Christian Counselors' Manual*. Briefly, homework is work assigned to counselees to do during the week between sessions. As faith without works is dead, so are commitments made in sessions not followed through afterwards. Homework not only helps assure the performance of such works but also speeds up counseling immeasurably.

success of counseling. There is, of course, nothing wrong with desiring relief – if God should so happen to grant it through counseling. However, when that is the top goal, rather than pleasing God – regardless of whether relief comes or not – counseling is sure to fail. Even when relief is the result, if God is not honored in obtaining it, your counseling will have failed. You will find that in all such cases you must take time to discuss counseling goals with your counselee in order to help him understand and frame biblical objectives. Otherwise, you will embark on a fruitless and sinful course of action. It is only when he understands and accepts the goal of putting God's will before his own that it is safe to proceed with counseling. Until such a time you should make re-negotiating his agenda your first and only counseling task. When he finally understands and truly makes God's agenda his own, then he will be ready for counseling about his presentation problems.

In order to achieve proper conditions for counseling, like those I have just mentioned, you may find it necessary to bring forth cogent biblical passages particularly pertinent to the matter and call him to repentance. Remember, repentance is a change of mind, precisely what you want. You are working for a *change* in his agenda. Don't forget that genuine repentance always issues in a change of behavior as well. So, you should see in him a new eagerness to please God by doing what He requires. Until you are able to minister the Word effectively so that this change occurs, as I said, it will be futile to try to counsel. But when there is true repentance you will discover not only a change in behavior, but also in attitude. A new holy seriousness should come over the counselee that was lacking before. That is because you will have emphasized, and he will have realized, the fact that the repentance is a transaction that occurred between him and God. *You* are but a catalyst who ministered the Word in the power of the Spirit Who, in turn, brought it about.

If God has touched your counselee's heart prior to his coming for counseling, (or after repentance such as that mentioned above) you will find counseling is able to move forward at a fairly rapid pace. Capitalize on this development. That is to say, when he is willing to put God first, you should be willing to help your counselee move forward rapidly. Take advantage of his readiness to tackle tasks – perhaps even more than you had planned for him. Don't stall, when you discover momentum building. Otherwise, you may throw cold water on his newfound fervor. Too many counselors think that they must reach some sort of rapport with a counselee beyond the commonalties that grow out of the use of the Scriptures. That is a grievous mistake. When your counselee is ready for help, give it to him. What you should strive for is rapport between him and God!

Sometimes, like those mentioned in the last chapter, your counselee may wish to substitute his own ways of dealing with his problem. Usually, because of his eagerness, these substitutes turn out to be short cuts. Forewarning about this usually gets results. If, however, it doesn't, direct, firm, confrontation about the seriousness of this pursuit ordinarily will achieve good results. If not, you may have to halt further counseling until the matter is resolved.

As always, send your counselee off with assignments that he is likely to succeed in doing. This will encourage him from the outset. However, you might attach some element that is probably a bit more difficult than, at this point, he can handle successfully. This will help cool down unruly enthusiasm on his part.

Other reasons, such as fear, may stand in the way of given assignments. These must be handled as I shall note presently in a following chapter. For now, in anticipation, read I John 4:18 where the Spirit reveals that love for God and one's neighbors is the antidote to fear.

Blessed is the counselor who finds a counselee anxious to do whatever God requires to solve his problem!

Shy

So far, we've considered some of those who are eager to be counseled. It is smooth sailing when they are in line with biblical concerns. However, such persons are a rare find. There are many who seem highly motivated, it is true, but balk as soon as they are confronted with biblical change. There may be many reasons for this. For instance, a counselee may stall because of fear, frequently because of the fear of consequences. In such cases, you will probe in order to discover what it is that your counselee fears and deal with it. Unpleasant tasks such as confessing sin and receiving the negative responses of others, the possible loss of a job, the estrangement of children or a spouse, the loss of money, may lead a counselee to dig in his heels. The list of fears that might be named could go on almost indefinitely. In such cases, you will deal with each cause particularly. But in all, you will surely want to encourage your counselee to "be strong and courageous," as Moses encouraged Joshua when faced with uncertainty and danger (Deuteronomy 31:23). Moreover, you will want to point out the appropriate passages of Scripture that pertain to the *particular* problem that the counselee has, since Paul tells us that it is the promises of God *in Scripture* that give hope and encouragement (read Romans 15:13, 4 in that order[1]). Even though you will encounter it regularly, there is one fear that is rarely addressed when considering the fear: *the fear of failure.*

---

1. In verse 13, the promise of abundant hope is given; in verse 4, the means of obtaining it – from Scripture – is set forth. One hope-giving passage frequently referred to by Nouthetic counselors is I Corinthians 10:13. The pamphlet entitled, *Christ and Your Problems,* which is an exposition of how God enables us to face problems, whatever they may be, is useful in helping such counselees.

The fear of failure itself may take on many different faces. As a matter of fact, it may relate to almost any activity you can name. Young people fear failing in college, newly-wedded husbands and wives may fear that their marriages will crumble, preachers may fear that they will not be able to live up to the expectations of a new congregation, even counselors may fear losing counselees if they tell them the hard truth. Again, the items on such a list might seem endless. But, of all the fears of failure that you will encounter in counseling, there is one that is hardly ever mentioned, let alone addressed. And when it is neglected, as it so often is, counseling will prove unsuccessful.

The fear of failing that I have in mind, is the fear of embarrassment. When there are so many ways of failing that might lead to embarrassment, don't you find it strange that so little attention is given to the matter? I do. Perhaps the major reason for this lack is that this fear may not be readily recognized. And the prime reason why it is not recognized is that it has been labeled with the innocuous tag – "shyness." You may also wonder, if, as I am contending it is so prevalent, why the Scriptures say nothing about the matter. After all, you will not find the word "shy" in Strong's concordance!

Well, as you will soon learn, when you counsel persons who are considered "shy," there is, indeed, a great deal in the Bible about them. The problem is that a misleading term, "shyness," has obscured the fact. "Shyness," so-called, is one form of what the Bible calls "pride."

You will make a cardinal mistake if you opt for a truncated view of pride. It is many-sided. Surely, you will have no difficulty identifying pride in the loud-mouthed boaster or the not-so-subtle braggart. You will easily identify the pride that dominates the life of the insufferable bore who can find nothing more interesting to talk about than himself. But you may wonder how a shy person, the outstanding characteristic of whom is unwillingness to push himself forward, can be said to be proud. He will rarely try new things, he will not participate in unfamiliar activities, he never seeks the limelight. Do not such persons rather suffer from low self-esteem? Are not wallflowers at parties who huddle in corners and politely decline when asked to play charades or some other game that places one in the spotlight anything but proud? The proud that you can easily recognize are the show-offs and loud talkers, but surely not the quiet mice who remain out of sight and hearing, whose presence is almost undetected. So people think.

And, so it would seem! That's the way many see things; and why, incidentally, such people are not helped when they come for counseling. At first blush (a word that appropriately describes them at times) the fearful proud seem to be anything but proud. Pride can be subtle – much more so than many realize. The unnoticed fact in the mislabeling of the fearful proud as "shy" is that they all have in common a fear of failing that would lead to embarrassment. "Above all, I must never attempt to do anything that might cause people to laugh at me, or that may lead them to call me incompetent," is the attitude behind their "shyness" mask.

It is such people who failed to make the cut for the team for one reason or another that afterward go around poo-pooing football. "It is only a fool who would waste his time watching such a stupid sport," they tell others, as they suck on sour grapes! It's such people who, having slipped often enough to obtain wet bottoms after their first time out on the ice, give up and never again attempt to learn to skate. Because people rarely do anything well without persistent practice in the face of difficulty and failure, they quit too soon. As a result, they back off from activity after activity until their horizons become very limited. Failure leading to embarrassment soon dominates their minds. Thus, this sinful approach to all activities that might possibly lead to failure also causes the fearful proud to shirk many responsibilities. More often than not, this avoidance habit stiffens into a life pattern,

"Low self-esteem?" Hardly. Just the opposite is true. The unspoken cause behind the failure of the fearful proud to attempt various activities, and the sour grapes attitude to which this leads, stems from the problem of too high a sense of self-esteem. "I'll not have people laughing at me or putting me down. So, I'll stay aloof from any and all activities that might occasion such indignities." That's the way pride takes hold of such people.

Actually, such pride comes from a failure to admit that one is a sinner and, as such, will fail often and sometimes seriously. While there is no excuse for such failure, neither is there any excuse for giving up on much in life out of pride. It is because of this pride that Christians often fail to pull their load in the church. They will neither discover, develop, or deploy such gifts, and the body suffers. They refuse to seize opportunities to advance at work because this may involve the possibility of failure. They refuse to develop new skills because they may be asked to use them in "risky" situations (risky, to them means the possibility of being embarrassed by failure of some sort). All of us imperfect creatures learn by successes and failures; but they refuse to do so. You could name a hundred situations in which fear of failure has shrunken their lives to the point of utter misery. *Safety* is their watchword. Always take the safe route – i.e., the one that safely leads around any and all possibilities of failure.

How is this attitude to be handled in counseling? Plainly, by exposing the truth behind the word "shyness." Sin is always "unfruitful." In II Peter 1:8 the apostle makes it clear that God expects us to enjoy the fruit that grows out of productive, biblical, Christian living. The Spirit produces this fruit through the application of His Word to our activities. But humility is the necessary quality of life that is consistent with the Spirit's activity. Indeed, God opposes the proud, but gives grace to the humble (I Peter 5:5). This fact must be presented with a force strong enough to lead to repentance. It isn't only sinful reluctance to do what God requires that ought to concern you, it is also the underlying pattern behind this reluctance. Unless it is rooted out and replaced with the fruitful plant of humility, more and more similar acts will continue to grow like noxious weeds. So, exposing the habitual dynamic behind the problem is necessary, but replacing it with acts calculated to help one grow must also be done. That will require acts fearfully, but faithfully, performed as home-work. Heavy coaching by you at first will be essential. Encouragement and hope must abound in sessions.[1] Pride has devastating effects on one's life. So, never fail to uncover it when it is present, and deal with it straightforwardly. There are few greater joys than to watch a shriveled up little soul blossom into a glorious flower. Your work with the sinfully shy will enable you to enter into their coming out into the sunshine.

---

1.   See my book, *Encouragement Isn't Enough*.

Interested, but Uncertain

People often come for help, but have reservations. This ambivalence is often noticeable from the outset. I am not referring to visible signs of the nervousness that most counselees have at their initial visit. Rather, what I have in mind is a discernible uncertainty that manifests itself in expressions of doubt or hesitation. One reason for this may be his uncertainty about you. There is nothing wrong about this unless you are counseling a long standing member of your flock. We're not speaking about a member who has recently joined the congregation, and has had only limited exposure to you. Those who have known you for years should be aware both of your competence, care, and reliability. For example, they should know that anything that they say privately in counseling sessions will not become an illustration for next week's sermon.

Sheep know and love their shepherd, and if you are a faithful one, they will trust you every bit as much as those white, fleecy, animals trust their shepherds. If the problem of uncertainty persists, however, you should immediately begin to do something about it. Perhaps you have not drawn close enough to your people. You may be (or may seem to them to be) standoffish even though in your heart this is the last thing that you'd want others to think. You know that you long to get close to the members of your flock, but your manner holds people at arm's length. If this is true, you need to determine to change your demeanor by making genuine attempts to rectify the situation. The closer relationship you long for will not develop unless you also make conscious efforts to become more accessible. In doing so, you may find it necessary to find ways to spend more warm, casual time with your members. But that is not the issue in this chapter. I mention it simply because reticence by such members who seek counsel may prove one way that a failure to connect with your people may come to light.

What shall we think about people who come to counseling with reservations and uncertainties? What is it that lies behind this? Let's consider two factors that may contribute to their uncertainty. People may be uncertain about your counseling method. Or, as I have suggested in the previous paragraph, they may be uncertain about your counseling ability. For the sake of simplicity, we shall suppose that the reticent counselee is not a member of your church. How can you reassure uncertain counselees who are unfamiliar (or reasonably unfamiliar) with you?

First, while a certain amount of uncertainty is understandable, excessive hesitancy is not. Whenever you detect more than usual apprehension, you need to discover what is behind it. Is it nothing more than the lack of familiarity that might be true of any such initial meeting? Some people are overly cautious whenever they find themselves in unusual circumstances. They always approach new relationships with extreme caution. Others have had bad experiences in the past and are on their guard. This is true particularly when they know that they are about to speak of intimate and difficult matters. They may have had bad experiences in the past, and don't want to be "burned" again. Or is there more to their uncertainty? Find out.

Perhaps your counselee has heard rumors about Nouthetic counseling. Many people, who know little or nothing about what a Nouthetic counselor does, nevertheless spread gossip because they have "heard" such and such about the method. There is a climate of opinion based upon hearsay rather than fact that, unfortunately, pervades certain Christian circles. Nouthetic counseling has become controversial because it challenged the psychological establishment in the church. As a result, those whose interests have been jeopardized have noised about various untruths concerning this biblical method. If this explanation is unearthed in discussion with your counselee, you will want to deal with it definitively before going further. You will want to discover exactly what it is that the would-be counselee has heard. Then you will be able to set his mind at rest by explaining the facts.

If a counselee openly expresses his uncertainty at the out-set of counseling, you may find yourself already ahead of the game. If he does not, but the uncertainty is discernible, you will have to bring the matter to the surface. Doing so usually isn't all that difficult. Simply questioning him about it usually is all that is needed. A question like, "You seem hesitant about beginning. Can you tell me why?" might suffice.

If the matter has to do with your competence as a counse-lor, the very best way to counter any such suspicions is to treat your counselee in a business-like manner. Initial, brief pleasantries ought to open every first session. Following these greetings, in most cases, you will want to move immediately to data gathering. You do not want to waste your counselee's valuable counseling time, as some do, by attempting to estab-lish rapport. Indeed, rapport is best attained by competent, friendly, business-like procedures on your part. So, unless your counselee's discomfort is excessive it is wise to turn immediately to gaining greater specificity about responses given on the PDI. Responses on the Inventory that are impre-cise or incomplete should lead you to ask for clarification. Having dealt with these, you will then move to the answers to the questions on the last page of the PDI. Doing so will launch you into counseling proper. Unless you detect your counselee dragging his feet during this initial fact-finding period you should not hesitate to continue to move forward. In most cases able, efficient handling of this initial stage will dispel questions about your competence.

If, however, you detect strong reticence remaining after doing the above, you should stop and openly address it: "Is there some fact of which you should make me aware before we go any further?" This, or some similar remark, may be all it takes to prick the blister. Having received a response that demands explanation, clarification, or refutation, you will be able to proceed once you have dealt with it. In cases where it is needed, do not fail to take the time to dispel the uncertainty. In the long run, by doing so, you will not lose time, but rather gain it. You don't want the actual counseling you are about to do to be hampered by some unsatisfied problem that has not been handled early on. Failure to take the time will slow down counseling in the remainder of the hour, and perhaps during several sessions to come. You don't want to drag a ball and chain about as you attempt to counsel. Counseling itself has enough difficulties that you don't need to carry any more burdens than are necessary into counseling sessions. So, at all costs, deal with uncertainties. Ignoring them can defeat your best efforts.

Counselors

Sometime or other (perhaps sooner than you might think) you will counselor a counselor. More likely than not he will be the pastor of a church. He may or may not be one who actively does much counseling. Although by calling themselves pastors, they ought to counsel; yet many preachers do not. So you will want to discover up front whether or not the man you are about to counsel is obedient to God in this respect. Is he, or is he not, a counseling pastor? Moreover, if he does do counseling you will want to discover what manner of counseling he engages in. Is it psychologically or biblically based? Or is it some sort of eclectic stew? How you go about counseling him will depend, to some extent, upon the answers to these questions.

If your counselee's training and practice is psychologically oriented, you will want to let him know at the outset that what you intend to say and do will be contrary to his practices. A brief rundown of what the procedures that you intend to follow may be necessary in order to give him a rough sketch of how you counsel. Doing so will enable him to determine whether or not he wants to proceed further. If you fail to inform him you may find it miserable going for both of you when counseling in days ahead, since both of you are likely to be pulling in opposite directions.

If, on the other hand, your counselee seldom (or never) counsels, you may need to admonish him, urging him to become a counseling pastor. But, probably, this admonition should be reserved for a later time, after successfully dealing with his problems. In some instances, a pastor who had no training in biblical counseling, once helped, may want to sit in on some of your counseling sessions to learn more about how to counsel biblically.

Other pastors may claim to do "biblical" counseling when, actually, they don't. It would be wise to examine exactly what they mean by that term since so much eclectic counseling (wrongly) sails under that flag. If you discover that he is actually eclectic, once more, I suggest openly comparing and contrasting your counseling approach with his. This ought to be done briefly, not in an extended manner, or with lengthy discussion. Your aim in doing so would be to make him aware of what will take place if he wishes to continue. There is no sense in getting into unnecessary difficulties two or three sessions later because of differences that he was unaware of at the outset.

Then, you must remember, there are pastors and counselors whose methodology is truly Nouthetic. In some instances, they may prove more difficult to counsel than others. In other cases, they may be the easiest of all. The attitude of such counselors largely will account for which of these two cases proves true. If a counselor comes with a know-it-all attitude or if he endeavors to take charge of counseling, you may be forced to halt proceedings to explain, clearly and calmly, but firmly, that these tactics must come to an end or they will hamper counseling. Often, the embarrassment factor may predominate: "Here I am a counselor, consulting a counselor!" The goal, if this seems to be the case, is to set him at ease: "At times we all need the help of others. Once, when I was having difficulty..." Such leveling of the playing field, so long as you don't tip it the other way, is helpful. But it must not eventuate in a lack of leadership on your past. At all times you must remain in charge of counseling sessions.

Having come to an understanding with a Nouthetic counselee, you can probably proceed apace. He will know the ropes. He knows about the PDI, the last three questions on the final page, the use of homework, the six-week checkup, and other practices common to our counseling. This should speed up counseling, reducing sessions by at least one or two. Time normally spent in explaining the procedures will be saved and gained. However, you must not fail to devote adequate time to his case. The temptation may be to do so and, indeed, he may encourage you to take shortcuts. Beware; most shortcuts turn out to be dead-ends.

When counseling a counselor, it will be wise to speak clearly at the outset not only about possible differences in counseling methodology, but also about the issues that I have just mentioned. The more clarity about your relationship roles in counseling that you can achieve, the better counseling will progress. So, absolute transparency should characterize all that you do and say.

Although, as I said, you ought to compare and contrast biblical methods with those of a psychologically-oriented or eclectically-oriented counselor, you should not become involved in an argument about them. Your counselee has come for help, not to discuss methodology. You have a way of offering help and he should either accept your counseling for what it is or it would be better not to begin. One concession you should definitely insist upon is that the Scriptures must have final say in all of the issues that arise.

This concession, of course, leads to the matter of theological differences. Because that is where difficulties, some of which may be extraneous to the counseling problem presented, may arise, you may find that these tend to obstruct progress. You do not want to reach an impasse if it is possible to avoid it. On the other hand, neither do you want such issues to emerge in later sessions when you have been making progress. I suggest laying them out early on in a *matter-of-fact* rather than *adversarial* manner: "You understand, of course, that I am a Calvinist," or "Counseling will proceed on the basis that no revelation outside of Scripture will be accepted." The attitude that I have in mind when I said "matter-of-fact" is one in which you assume, rather than argue your theological stances. When handled that way, usually in a one-or-two-sentence exchange is all that is necessary to clarify matters so as to nullify future argumentation. The counselor came to you and he should expect you to stick to your guns! You will feel much more confident about how you counsel when you have removed the threat of possible theological arguments that may, other wise, be hanging over both of your heads. That is one reason for anticipating and confronting differences up front. Doing so should put both you and the counselee at ease. In all instances, I urge you not to hesitate to maintain utter openness about such things. Beating about the bush can only create unnecessary tension for both you and your pastor-counselee.

When counseling a counselor, you will also have to avoid being intimidated by him. Many counselors, especially if they belong to the Nouthetic School, are strongly directive. They develop strong personalities and, unlike other counselees, may attempt (often unconsciously) to take charge of the session. But, as I noted previously, you may not allow him to gain control. If you do, you may find it difficult to regain it. If the counselor-counselee succeeds in grasping hold of the reins, you can expect him to destroy counseling and, at the same time, to lose confidence in you. This, indeed, may even morph into disrespect. So, be sure that you remain in charge at all times. If, despite your best efforts to avoid it, your counselee becomes overbearing, insisting on having his own way or attempting again and again to take over the session, you will have to bring counseling to a halt. At that point, depending on how serious his constant interference is, you may have to confront him about his attitude, telling him to desist or, in the likelihood of his continuing, you will have to terminate counseling altogether. Of course, you will do all that is possible to avoid reaching this impasse. But because of his obstinacy it may not be possible to continue.

Lazy and Indifferent

Many problems that counselees bring to the counseling table are due to irregular life patterns. These are of their own making. Moreover, not only are such patterns the genesis of their difficulties, but these same tendencies also become impediments to progress in counseling. For that reason, it is vital for the counselor to be able to recognize these destructive, habitual ways of life and, having done so, to learn how to deal with them.

How may you detect laziness and indifference in your counselee? Fundamentally, in two ways:

1. Through your counselee's expressed attitudes;

2. Through his approach toward homework assignments.

First, let's consider expressed attitudes. By "attitude" I mean the state of mind that one exhibits toward certain persons and circumstances. In some cases, one's state of mind may be so uniform that it extends to all of life. Obviously, a counselor will not be able to observe how his counselee responds to many situations, but he can listen to what he says in sessions, how he says it, and take note of the attitudes that he expresses during counseling itself. Often observations by others (spouses, for instance) will add immeasurably to the knowledge you need. But this must always be confirmed by your own observations. You must be very cautious about observations made by others, knowing that, frequently, one party will attempt to prejudice you against the other. But when your own conclusions from what you see and hear in counseling coincide with those of another party, that will often strengthen your understanding of your counselee's lifestyle.

A lazy person's attitude is a foolish state of mind that causes him to avoid the expenditure of effort. A counselee may give you bogus reasons (excuses) for his behavior in an attempt to escape doing anything that even smells like work. These ploys will often become evident when you explain to him that the only way out of some dilemma is by exerting various efforts to change. A lazy state of mind, given time to work itself out in all of life, may so engulf a counselee that he will abandon even simple, necessary functions. The luxury of excessive sleep, as well as other characteristics of a leisurely manner of life that he can ill afford to pursue, will manifest themselves in the pursuit of pleasures that require no effort on his part – eating, watching TV, and the like. Responsible activity will be laid aside whenever it intrudes on lethargy. I call laziness "foolish" because that is how the Scriptures characterize the lifestyle of a lazy person. Indeed, it is important to notice that God consistently exposes their transparently outrageous excuses, sleepy indulgence, and pitiful inability to perform the simplest tasks by poking fun at the lazy. See the following passages in Proverbs: 6:6–11; 10:4, 26; 19:15; 22:13; 24:30–34; 26:13–16. In these passages not only does God mock lazy persons, but also shows the dire consequences of their irresponsible attitudes toward life.

Laziness will become apparent as lazy counselees fail to do their homework. "It was too hard, there were too many interruptions, I didn't understand it" – he will give you these, and a bucketful of other, excuses that fail to hold water when examined. You see, he will not do homework because it is home-*work*! Since work is taboo to him, he'd rather excuse his behavior than modify it. He may even expend effort in the attempt to find ways of avoiding homework. You may exhort him until the cows come home, but – short of repentance and help to change – he will continue to find ways around making the effort to comply with your assignments. These factors, so graphically illustrated in the verses referenced above (the rusty door turning in its bed, the inability to lift a hand to one's mouth to eat, the lion in the street that keeps one from going to work, and so on) will in one modern form or other come alive in your presence in the counseling room. Excuses, excuses, excuses! That's the order of the day for the lazy.

When confronting a lazy person you want to be sure of your facts. It is possible to characterize a person as lazy when his reasons (strange as they may seem) may be legitimate. Thoroughly check out the reasons he offers to make sure they are not excuses, before you label him with the biblical epithet. But when you have verified your suspicions to be fact, you should confront him as Scripture does. His sin is treated both with sarcasm and with a recital of the consequences of prolonged laziness. Because God does, following His example, you too should use those sharp weapons in the war against laziness. You will have to devise ways of using them most effectively. Here is one way that you may want to use in helping a lazy counselee overcome his laziness. Simply say, as you write and hand him a note, "OK. This week I don't want to burden you, so here's your homework." On the note you will have written something like the following:

Get up this morning if you have the strength.

Brush a tooth, but don't overdo it.

Eat one or two Cheerios, but take your time.

If that, or a similar homework assignment, given with a grin doesn't make your point, you should move to the serious consequences of a life of laziness as depicted in the overgrown farmer's field and the other pertinent verses listed above. As you hand him the facetious assignment, you might want to add, "Carry this note home and place it in some conspicuous place where you can see it every day – think you can handle that?" Remember, God's way of defeating laziness is to expose its stupidity and disastrous consequences. Use both of these tools. The goal in doing so, is of course, to bring your counselee to repentance through shame.[1] Repentance is a change of mind about an ungodly lifestyle leading to a change in living that honors God.

---

1. In bringing Christians to repentance, Paul does not hesitate to shame them (cf. II Thessalonians 3:14).

What about indifferent people? To be indifferent is not to care about something or someone. Indifference may have come from at one time "writing off" that which a counselee now shows little or no interest in. What he deems unimportant, peripheral, or downright wrong can cause him, henceforth, to treat it with indifference. Having once distanced himself from it, the indifferent person keeps aloof from whatever he has rejected, or never thought worth showing any interest in. While he may not turn up his nose to it, he will turn his back on it. To be indifferent is to be distanced in one's attitude from the object, topic, or person considered not worth giving it the time of day.

Indifference in counseling is manifested by an obvious lack of concern about some important issue that is vital to obtaining the help that your counselee so desperately needs. You would think that he would want to be deeply involved in anything that might help him eliminate his difficulties, but his detached state of mind deflects his concern elsewhere. If you haven't encountered it already, you will find indifferent persons so detached from truth and righteousness that they may even turn aside from Scripture. They take the tack, "Oh that doesn't pertain to me," and go on ignoring biblical truth. The attitude shown by such persons, expressed or otherwise, is "don't bother me with something so irrelevant."

What causes indifference? Various reasons may be adduced. But they will all boil down to one thing: at some time or other, he adopted it as a strategy. He decided to avoid being called upon to assume difficult or unpleasant responsibilities. So, he struck a pose (which, in time, became an attitude) that it did not interest him. Your indifferent counselee may not have ever wanted your counsel in the first place. If he was dragged into counseling by a spouse, a parent, or some other interested party, he is there under duress. Resorting to his usual stance, he pleads unconcern – counsel is not for him because he doesn't need it. A competent counselor will ferret out whatever led (or leads) a counselee to take a stand like this. Having done so (and it would take another chapter to discuss the various ways to go about it[1]), the counselor's next challenge is to attempt to convince his counselee of the importance of the matter that he has been snubbing. There are two biblical approaches to doing so: to inform him about how his own welfare depends upon taking interest, and, what is of greater importance, to clearly set forth from the Scriptures how what is important to God ought to be important to him. He will try to side step that discussion, naturally, but you must not allow him to do so. Bringing cogent arguments from pertinent passages of Scripture (one or two that you bore down upon) is the way to accomplish this. You may describe these three points as:

1. Setting forth the dire consequences of the counselee's indifference;

2. Dramatically setting forth the large benefits that accrue from taking interest;

3. Setting forth God's displeasure with his present attitude.

Points one and three are explicit enough. But point two may need some explanation. When I say, "dramatically setting forth" the benefits of getting on board, I mean just that. Nothing less than something so dramatic that it cannot fail to gain attention will serve your purpose. The prophets who were called to do dramatic things in order to bring indifferent Israelites to repentance demonstrate the fact. When God wanted to get attention, He often called upon a prophet to do outrageous things such a marry a harlot, build and dig through a clay fort, and lie on his side for prolonged periods of time. Indifferent counselees must be drawn in by getting their attention.

Wives, who were unable to move their counselees out of their chairs to get counseling, have often done so by threatening divorce. Obviously, I cannot commend their action, but I

---

1. All of which involve nothing new that hasn't already been thoroughly discussed in the data gathering section of *The Christian Counselors' Manual*.

mention it to show how a dramatic action (or even the threat of it) can penetrate indifference. There may come a time when the only means that a counselor has to move an indifferent counselee to action is to threaten church discipline. Other less threatening, but equally effective, dramatizations may be devised. A person, who has already experienced very deleterious effects from his past indifference before repentance, may be urged to confront and talk to your counselee about it. In doing so, he should spell out in vivid detail how it harmed his life and, in particular, his relationship to the Lord. Other means, suited to your counselee and his circumstances, will come to mind for you when you begin to think of the need for dramatization. To indifferent persons, truly actions may speak louder than words.

John the Baptist came on the scene, dressed like Elijah, calling for repentance, and demonstrating its necessity by the demand from God to be baptized. His very successful ministry of awakening the Jews for the coming of Jesus Christ was buttressed by both a negative and positive message. He heralded the coming of a Savior, the Lamb of God Who would take away the sins of people from all over the world, while (at the same time) warning that the ax was laid at the root of the Jewish tree, thereby forecasting the destruction of Jerusalem. That people were awakened from indifference is clear in that "all Jerusalem and all Judea" went out into the desert to hear him and be baptized (Mark 1:5). He preached the coming of the Kingdom of heaven and, at the same time, urged people to flee from the wrath to come. Putting the two together, the joy of the one and the horror of the other was calculated to awaken every sort of indifferent person. Because of John's dramatic ministry, many believed in Jesus when He appeared. Of course, the leadership of the nation did not, and those who followed them went into destruction such as had never been known previously. He warned against the wrath to come. The historian, Josephus, who was on the scene, tells the story of mothers boiling and eating their children because of hunger, and the rest of the horror that was experienced in 70AD. Warnings given to the indifferent should be explicit.

In general, then, it is wise to be able to recognize laziness and indifference in people who come for counseling. You must help them in spite of themselves. That makes counseling difficult – but challenging. Remembering how so many Jews were saved by John's dramatic ministry should encourage you to urge God's hope, warnings, and demands upon such counselees. God's message will awaken the indifferent and enliven the lazy when, in His providence, He determines for it to do so. One thing both the indifferent and the lazy have in common is the self-destructive nature of their attitudes. These people, in particular, need to be saved from themselves. Knowing this, it is your privilege to rescue them before it is too late.

Disorganized and Undisciplined

The two problems are often congenial bedfellows. Undisciplined people usually are also disorganized. On the other hand, it is possible that disorganized people may be undisciplined in some areas while disciplined in areas not pertaining to order. But, mostly, where you find the one, you will also find the other. The issue that must be dealt with when helping counselees with these problems, therefore, will also necessitate learning discipline – at least in some areas. Usually, orderliness must be newly minted since it has not been the coin of the realm for such counselees.

Let's consider disorganized living first. Frequently, you will find that this way of life is highly destructive to counselees and to those who must associate with them. It is rare that this self-destructive way of living does not spill out into the lives of others. What does it look like and how may it be handled in a biblical fashion? Sometimes disorganized living is overtly the principal presentation problem. More often, it will be found to be a complicating problem that grows along the way as a counselee fails to handle other problems properly. Sometimes it accompanies a "giving up" on some matter which, in discouragement, leads to giving up on others. You will often find behind disorder, therefore, discouragement and even depression. The latter may lead to the former, but usually it is the other way around.

Disorder has become more-or-less overt when a businessman or housewife allows work to pile up and things get lost or, otherwise, end up out of place. Such persons, it seems, have never heard the expression, "A place for everything, and everything in its place." Nor do they know "A time for everything and everything in its time." They are accomplished at putting things off, misplacing items, not keeping appointments, over-scheduling, not scheduling, and numerous other such irregularities. There are homes where you literally must

walk through aisles between piles of junk, heaps of maga-
zines, newspapers, and the like. There are offices where
important documents are displaced, missing, or destroyed.
There are students who miss-locate class assignments, and
put off studying for tests until the very last minute. Disorder
and disorganization have led to failing tests, to losing jobs,
and to the breaking up of families. Too often disorder is made
light of until its sad effects become burdensome. It is a condi-
tion that may lead to serious consequences, as I said, but
worse, it leads to disapproval by God. Disorder is sin!

Consider I Thessalonians 4:12 where God tells the Thessalonians that they must learn to lead an orderly life. Commen-
tators differ about the cause of the disorder in the young
congregation (whether or not false teaching about the coming
of Christ may have led to it), but regardless of the cause it is
clearly denounced as more than a trivial problem in God's
eyes. Disorder was severely upsetting this infant church. The
word, *euschemonos* (translated "decently") used in I Thessalonians 4:12, is the same word that occurs in I Corinthians
14:40 where it is connected with *taxis*, a Greek term that has
to do with such ideas as lining up troops in order.[1] Together,
we translate them as "decently and in order." This combination of words indicates that *orderliness* is the *decent* way in
which God expects us to live. Disorder, in other words, is lack
of that which has beauty, and therefore, is indecent in His
sight.

Disorder is a style of sinful living that you will have to
confront. In helping counselees become orderly, as in all problems involving learning something new, disorder must be
replaced by the hard work of discipline. Those who don't want
to put forth this effort may attempt to "laugh it off" as not all
that important but, since God doesn't seem to think that it is
funny, you may not allow them to dismiss the issue in this
lighthearted manner. Don't listen to those who say such
things as "Well, that's just old Joe for you." Tell them it may

---

1.   The term *euschemonos*, in some contexts, can also mean "beauty."

be so, but it's old Joe that God wants to change for His sake. The matter is not indifferent.

Well, how do you go about helping the disordered? Take a second look at how Paul did. First, he exposed it as indecent in God's sight – an unworthy spectacle for God to look at. Conversely, He called for beauty in the way we live and do things. He showed the deleterious effects of disorder upon others in the church and upon unbelievers as well. You must similarly exhort counselees.

Disorder in Christians reflects poorly upon God Himself, as it is repulsive to unbelievers as well. In I Corinthians 14:23, disorder is said to bear a bad testimony to the lost which, in the case discussed, might lead them to conclude from the Corinthians' disorderly use of spiritual gifts that Christians were crazy. Note also I Corinthians 14:23 and 14:39, in which God makes it plain that He expects order since He, Himself, is a God of order.

Disorder, as noted above, is regularly associated with lack of discipline, the latter usually leading to it. Lack of discipline means failure by your counselee to train himself to habitually do what God expects of him. When God commands "discipline yourself for godliness," he uses the word from which our term "gymnasium" comes. It was a word that referred to the training that athletes undergo so as to acquire various skills and abilities. This training includes regularity, consistency, and strenuous effort. Discipline, in every area of life, requires the presence of these three elements. Where they are absent, discipline is absent.

Undisciplined living may characterize your counselee's life. When it does, it will be his principal problem. When it is not so widespread, it should nevertheless be dealt with because it is a complicating problem that displeases God. No one disciplines himself in the abstract. As Paul put it, discipline was "for" the purpose of godliness.[1] You too, must discipline counselees for "godliness," but remember godliness

---

1. For more detail, see my booklet, *Godliness Through Discipline.*

involves many things. The rest of the letter that Paul wrote to Timothy specifies what he must do to become godly. You too, must get down to particulars with your counselees. Take one item at a time, and after he has habituated several, he will be able to generalize the practices learned to other areas of his life on his own. You will know that he is ready to do so when you see him make and stick to important changes, and when he can articulate the principles whereby he was able to attain and maintain these changes. Throughout the process, offer close monitoring to be sure that he continues regularity, consistency and effort. You may object that this is "works." Of course it is works – works that grow out of faith, commitment, and the power of the Spirit working to produce His fruit in the counselee by means of His word (cf. Philippians 2:13).

Stubborn

There is a fine line between stubbornness, on the one hand, and perseverance, determination, and conviction on the other. People with any of the last three attitudes, however, can easily cross the line into stubbornness. This may be imperceptible to those who do, although normally it isn't to others. It is the counselor's duty to enlighten his counselee about the matter since, for the most part, others will fail to do it. Normally, the task, like so many others a counselor must undertake, isn't very pleasant.

If there is a thin line, how can you tell the difference between stubbornness and the other attitudes mentioned above? Since stubbornness is a pejorative term, and the other three commendable, the ability to distinguish between and correctly classify each person is significant. How may you, as a counselor, faced with someone you suspect needs to acknowledge and deal with his stubbornness do so?

Pharaoh was stubborn in the face of unmistakable evidence that he was wrong and unable to thwart the power of God. Yet, he hung on – and on, and on! Truly, if ever there was a demonstrable case of stubbornness, his was it. He refused to bow to Jehovah when He demanded, "Let My people go" (Exodus 5:1; 7:16; 8:1, 20; 9:1, 13). Instead, he hardened his heart. When refusals were followed by manifestations of divine power, he relented. But, stubborn to the core, he went back on his permission after things cooled down. In the long run, his stubborn attitude meant not only losing the battle with Jehovah, but also losing his army in the river. Stubbornness is best understood, it would appear, as beginning with one person's foolish unwillingness to agree with another. It is an irresponsible and unreasonable unwillingness against overwhelming evidence to admit that he is wrong. And, you will observe that, even when admitting to the fact, a truly stubborn person may still stand pat.

According to the other half of the biblical story, not only did the opponents of God's people act stubbornly, Israel itself had great problems with stubbornness. This was so large a sin that occurred so frequently, they had to be continually rebuked for it. It was so common that they were nicknamed a "stiff-necked" people (Exodus 32:9; 33:5; Deuteronomy 9:6, 13; II Chronicles 30:8; Acts 7:51). This name is a common designation for stubborn people. Spicq writes:

> The metaphor of the neck (Hebrew *orep*), the part of the animal body "involved in the expression" is taken from the draft animal whose efforts to resist are located in the neck. When the horse or ass refuses to go on, it tightens or stiffens its neck.[1]

Like the recalcitrant animal, counselees may persist in what they do, refuse to acknowledge God's truth and, when presented with overwhelming biblical evidence, stiffen until brittle and refuse to concede a jot or tittle. When a counselee digs in his feet, and will not budge, the counselor must be ready to deal with this. How does he do so when a counselee says, "Sorry, pastor, but I'm afraid that's how it will be and neither you nor my wife are going to talk me out of it?" How will he handle a person who persists in spending money that she doesn't have on clothes and jewelry and all sorts of trinkets?

The first thing that a counselor faced with similar circumstances must do is to ascertain whether the stubbornly resistant counselee has clearly in his mind what it is that he is resisting. Frequently counselees do not. Counselees are notorious for mishearing, misunderstanding, engaging in selective hearing, and the lot. If this turns out to be the case, it is the counselor's duty (and his relief) to clarify whatever the mistake may have been. In most instances, when the matter has

---

1. Ceslas Spicq, *Theological Lexicon of the New Testament*, Vol. 2 (Peabody, Mass.: Hendrickson Publishers, 1994), p. 360.

been adequately cleared up resistance melts away. So, always begin with verification and clarification. Verify that the counselee understands, and if he doesn't – clarify!

But if the counselee knows perfectly well what it is that he is stubbornly refusing to do or concede, the counselor must bring counseling to a halt. His only concern at that point is whether or not the counselee is willing to acknowledge that he is refusing God – not merely the counselor. If he says, in effect, "I know what God wants, but I won't do it," (or however he phrases it), your approach should abruptly shift from an educational level to an exhortational one. You should ask plainly, "Are you telling me that no matter what God says about this you refuse to do it?" Having received an affirmative reply (possibly after putting the question in several forms in response to shifty, evasive replies) it is time to explain the consequences of openly defying God. Some of these may occur in divine providence as in James 5:19, 20 or, perhaps, by the church using its binding and loosing power to dismiss him from its membership (Matthew 18:15ff). This power was given at the official inception of the New Testament church (John 20:21–23). You must threaten to put him out of the church (into Satan's hands, as required by the Savior Whose church it is) only after copiously explaining all that is involved in dismissal. For information on the details of Church discipline, see my book, *The Handbook of Church Discipline*. After explaining everything as fully as possible, you should close the session and ask him to think carefully about what you said before giving his final answer. At whatever point that answer is forthcoming – or when he refuses to hear further exhortation – the process of Church discipline should be instituted.

You must be careful not to be nasty in exhorting the counselee, but lovingly serious. It should be done with genuine concern. It is a fearful thing to hand an erring brother over to Satan (the effect of putting one out of the church, as the Apostle put it). Your exhortation ought to reach so far as to even *implore* the counselee to repent and follow the Word of

God. Stubbornness cannot be tolerated because God does not tolerate it; righteousness cannot be compromised because God won't allow it. While the stubborn person remains glued to the spot, a faithful counselor will move heaven and earth in every biblically responsible way to help him change his mind. But he must not retreat from fundamental biblical requirements.

When Paul told the Corinthians that he would become all things to win all sorts of men, he was talking about going to every sort of legitimate length to do so. He would penalize himself, bear up under every sort of inconvenience, and so forth. He didn't care about what it meant to himself; he would take it on the chin. But one thing he would not do, and that is to compromise his message. That must remain fast. And he would steadfastly see that it did.

So, how does a counselor treat a stubborn counselee? In summary, as God does. He admonishes; He disciplines. His church must do the same. A counselor will give some time for reflection and repentance, but then, if there is no change, he institutes church discipline. Stubbornness is a form of rebellion against God that may not be permitted by God's church.

Now, of course, we all have rebellious tendencies left over from our pre-Christian life. The difference between the stubborn counselee that I have been describing and the rest of us who sin in this manner is that, at length, we recognize our sinful ways, regret them, and repent. Stubborn counselees do not; they refuse to budge. They deliberately refuse to submit to God. That is their distinguishing characteristic. But, thank GOD, He has a way of using His Word, when properly ministered, to soften hard hearts and relax stiff necks. God can change even the most rebellious Christian. And, take heart. That is what happens in most cases.

Complainers and Whiners

Both complainers and whiners are hard to take. Ask them politely, "How are you today?" and you get a ten-minute recital of all their ills and misfortunes. Most people try to avoid them whenever possible. At the very least, they are careful about greetings, "Nice to see you," works better than "How are you?" they soon discover! But this social problem isn't the main issue. Usually, it is merely a matter of insensitive indiscretion on their part but, of course, it can also signal a problem with self-centeredness as well. But that is for discussion at another place.

Complaining, of all sorts, is sin. It is sin because it is an objection to how God is running His universe. The complainer "knows better" than God about how things ought to be done – he would like to have charge of God's providence so that he could arrange things his way! Granted, he may not see this but, ultimately, complaints about the weather, one's health, the boss, and other people, are also complaints against God. He could have made you taller, given you richer parents, enabled you to make more money – you name it. The danger in all complaining, then, is simply this: people think, "God could have arranged things differently, but he didn't – and I don't like it!"

But if I Corinthians 10:9–13 says anything at all, it says this: You may not like things as they are, but neither does God like your complaining about His providence (v. 5). Indeed, He tells us that He left an entire generation of Israelites dead in the desert because of their idolatry *and their complaining*. Paul's commentary on this Old Testament account is that it was written "for our admonition." It is not merely a story to read for its interest value; it is there to warn and change believers today!

Since this is true, it is incumbent upon biblical counselors to show complaining counselees what dire effects can come from a lifestyle of challenging God's wisdom. What He doesn't like, He eventually destroys; that's one message of I Corinthians 10. Thankfully, it isn't the only message. Before judging, God mercifully explains, warns, admonishes and even pleads with His people to repent and begin to live as they should. He expects us to thankfully receive whatever comes from His hand, knowing that for His people, "God makes everything work together for the good of those who love Him" (Romans 8:28).

Tell this to your counselees and listen to their responses. Some will ask how a person can be thankful that he has cancer and not complain about it. Others will argue that if you are not talking nonsense, you are talking about impossibilities. The first group will be anxious to hear your explanations about how to go about handling things that they don't like. They are malleable, will hear you out, and will change – usually to their eternal benefit. The second will argue and dissent from what you say. They are the one's I wish to deal with now.

When a counselee says, "But you don't understand, preacher. Nobody has had to face a problem like the one I just described to you," stop him in his tracks and slowly read out loud I Corinthians 10:13. That verse gives the lie to his excuse. It will silence many complainers that you have to deal with. It is also a verse that graciously offers hope for those in trial. God reveals in it three facts about His providence that we might not have known otherwise. Here is the blessed assurance He offers:

1. Counselee, you will never face a trial that others have not successfully faced before you. Your problem is not unique.

2. God faithfully promises not to allow you to be tested beyond what you are able to bear – as long as you handle it His way.

3. The test will come to an end. Knowing that should enable you to endure it.

With promises like these, based (as Paul says) on God's faithfulness, how can there ever be a valid reason to complain?

Whining is a particularly heinous form of complaining. Those who whine are seeking sympathy. What makes that so egregious is that the whiner is out there actively recruiting others to join in his whining – or at least to assent to it. He is enlisting others to join him in sinning against God by complaining about His providence.

It isn't necessary, however, for a counselee to whine in order to win others over to his nefarious cause. Many a business, home, or church has been seriously disrupted by complainers. They spread their insidious disease among the members of the body, thus causing many others to become infected with it. Complaining is comparable to a communicable disease that we must stop before everyone comes down with it. The old (and still effective) method of treating it is by isolating the carrier. Typhoid Mary must be kept away from the rest of the body – or they must be kept from her. Either she must submit to God's cure for the disease (repentance leading to gratitude rather than complaint) or be removed from the rest. Repentance is the only known medicine that will work. It consists of acknowledging the sin, seeking forgiveness, and replacing complaint with thankfulness. If you don't deal with a complainer (to change the metaphor), you will soon see that he has invited a number of others to join him in holding pity parties.

Think of it – because God was displeased with complainers who would not repent, He wiped out an entire generation of people! That tells you how "displeased" He is with complaining. Complaining goes back to the Garden of Eden. Satan complained about God's restriction on the tree of the knowledge of good and evil. And this complaint about God's stinginess had its effect on others – Adam and Eve and the entire human race! Complaining, in the presence of the pristine Garden – think of it! How ungrateful can man be? Having been faced with his sin, Adam complained about Eve, and then Eve complained about the serpent. I guess there was no one left for the snake to complain about! But it is apparent how easily the disease spread.

When you think about it, Adam complained even though he had absolutely no problems! All was perfect. "But I do have problems," I can hear someone protest. Yes, you do – your problem came from Adam. But if you are a Christian, you also have blessings and the certainty of a better Eden for eternity! Thank God for the many blessings that you already have from God's hand – and stop complaining.

"But everyone complains," counselees will argue. Admit it. Tell them that at times you catch yourself doing so. But don't allow them to justify their sin by this ploy.

Explain, "When I realize how foolish and how sinful my complaining is, I also remember that Romans 8:28 hasn't been removed from the Bible and I am ashamed and deal with my sin. Moreover, I am working on the problem." If, indeed, that is the truth in your case, as it ought to be. At present, I am in pain most of the day. I have asked God for relief, but He hasn't seen fit to grant it. So be it. Now, I have something to constantly remind me to accept the pain as an aid to my sanctification as I seek to handle it the way God wants me to.

A counselor should take much the same tack in helping complaining Christians. When he does so, and they learn to handle problems and difficulties as a test through which to learn patience and endurance, they will be better off – and so will those around them!

Now, failure to complain doesn't mean that you may not ever express the fact that something is wrong. Of course not! But it does mean that you must not go about complaining about it. You should seek to remedy it. Upon failure to be able to do so, you must accept it (at least temporarily) as from God, and learn to use the problem as an aid to Christian growth. It is not sin for me to take biblically legitimate means to eliminate my pain. But until it is eliminated (if it ever is) I should profit from it spiritually. Complaining is a sinful wasting of time and energy that is utterly unprofitable. Make that point to counselees.

Critical

Before I begin, let me assure you that if you are one of them, you'll certainly find fault with this article!

It doesn't take unusual powers to find something or someone to criticize. After all, ours is a broken world filled with sinners. Sinners sin, and their sin messes up both the tasks they pursue as well as the lives that they live. But there is a difference between the person who goes about *finding* fault and the one who more-or-less stumbles upon it. Moreover, there is such a thing as helpful criticism and the opposite kind of criticism. And, to cap it all, to have a critical eye for error and wrongdoing so as to not fall into it, is the duty of every believer in Jesus Christ. That kind of critical attitude is not the same as hankering for something to criticize.

The scriptures clearly distinguish between right and wrong, truth and error, righteousness and evil, as well as a host of other opposite absolutes. There are no shades of moral gray; God doesn't grade on a continuum. So, we must be sure that in attempting not to be critical, in the bad sense of the word, we do not become lax in "distinguishing the things that differ" (Philippians 1:10).

Elsewhere, I have spoken of the fine line that divides persistence from stubbornness. Here is, likewise, such a line running between criticism and criticism – so fine that many fail to see it when they cross over the line. For a preacher to be critical of views that demand examination because members of his congregation are being influenced by them is a duty that he will shirk only to the detriment of the flock.

In Hebrews 5:11–14, the writer chides second generation Jewish Christians for becoming "dull" in hearing. Because they have become lax about the study of God's Word, their spiritual, critical capabilities had become dull (the word is used sometimes in Hellenistic literature of those who are comatose). As a result, the members of this Hebrew-Christian church had problems discerning between truth and error. And, as a result, they were coming to doubt their faith in Jesus Christ as Savior. In describing the problem, the writer used the word *aistheterion,* which refers to the capacity to distinguish one thing from another. In this case, truth from error, good from evil. So, it is certain that there is such a thing as developing a good, necessary capacity for critical judgment. Failure to maintain it was rightly criticized by the writer of Hebrews.

But there is also such a thing as becoming a grumbler, discontented with everything and everyone. The grumbler's views and desires must be acknowledged as right. Otherwise, he will criticize. There was a group of false teachers like this in the church to which Peter and Jude wrote (see II Peter 3:3; Jude 16). True, these were false teachers but, sadly, Christians also can fall into similar patterns. In writing to the Thessalonians, Paul warns against people who were upsetting the church. They refused to work, had time on their hands, and were disturbing the peace of the infant congregation by their idle talk and gossip (see II Thessalonians 3:6–12). In a powerful passage, Paul wrote:

> Whoever teaches differently and doesn't agree with the wholesome words of our Lord Jesus Christ and the teaching that is in keeping with godliness is conceited, understands nothing. He has an unhealthy desire for discussions and controversies over words, from which come envy, strife, blasphemies, suspicion, evils, incessant wranglings by persons with corrupted minds..."
>
> I Timothy 6:3, 5a

Notice the words, "unhealthy desire for discussions and controversies" and "incessant wranglings." That description tells you a lot about people who enjoy criticizing others. The tricky thing is, of course, that when you deal with such people, you must sort out who is the one who is causing the controversy. Both will accuse the other. And it is true that in this passage Paul takes a side against such persons. It would have been easy for those who were the perpetrators to claim that Paul and Timothy were the ones causing trouble, since Paul was critical of their activities. One fact, however, stands out – the teaching that is proper is the one that is in keeping with "godliness." That is how the two parties in any "he said/she said" controversy may be distinguished. Ask, "Who is helping and who is hindering the growth and ministry of God's people?" Whose words are "wholesome" and "healthy" in their effects on the body? Those with a critical spirit cause wranglings, controversies, and trouble for everyone. He whose spirit is proper heals rather than hurts.

Troublesomely critical counselees will probably come for counseling because they have not been able to get along with others. They must learn to examine their ways. If they are upsetting families, causing disruption, threatening schism, they must be dealt with summarily (Titus 3:10). Unless repentant, they must not be allowed to go on with such activities. Unfounded, unnecessary criticism must be opposed, and the people who engage in it must be exposed and (if unrepentant after confrontation) must be disposed of.

How should they be confronted? Again, as you speak to the critical brother or sister, point out the effects of his criticism as Paul does. But be careful about how you do so. Surely, you must speak to him with a very different attitude than the one that he manifests. A cool, unemotional, factual, caring approach is called for; one that doesn't invite more argumentation. Why so? Because it is right. But also, if you don't, you can be almost certain that you will become the latest recipient of your counselee's criticism. It's not that you are seeking to avoid difficulties for yourself but, rather, that if he becomes antagonistic toward you, you will not be able to help him. Agree with his critical assessment of things when he is correct (it may take some probing and investigation to assess matters), but then help him to deal with his attitude toward error in others, and toward the church in general. Point out, for instance, how the apostle Paul gave the Corinthians time to repent rather than coming down hard on them (II Corinthians 1:23–2:4). He could have made a beeline for Corinth to correct their faults, but, instead, he gave them space to see if they, themselves, would deal with their problems. Had they failed to do so, you can be sure he would have intervened (I Corinthians 13:1, 2). But notice how he warned, then gave time to see if it was heeded. He demonstrated how patience, at the right time and place, can win out over criticism. This must have been difficult for him since, remember, at the time, Paul was under intense criticism from false apostles who claimed that he was a fraud (I Corinthians 9:1ff).

It isn't possible to free every counselee from his sin. Those who criticize are especially difficult to help because of their tendency to criticize you and the counsel you offer. But the God Who converted and humbled the Pharisee Paul can bring even highly critical counselees to their knees. And that – as in the situation at Corinth – is exactly what they need.

Judgmental

"Don't judge, or you will be judged." Matthew 7:1

"Make a righteous judgment." John 7:24

There is no contradiction between these two statements. They both command us not to judge; they both tell us to judge. In Matthew, Jesus warns us that others (perhaps referring also to God as well as man) will judge us in the same way that we judge them. So we ought to be both cautious and slow about how we judge them. In John 7, He warns against superficial judgment ("according to what appears on the surface"). Judgment, to be "righteous" (i.e., "rightly" administered), must go deeper. There is usually more than that which appears at first. Judgmental persons fail to heed Jesus' warnings, or to follow His directions.

Should one simply avoid judging since it is so risky? No. All must judge (indeed, all *will*). Look again at Matthew 7. You are to judge, Jesus says, with an eye from which a log has been removed. You must judge – but rightly! Then, He goes on to say it will be possible to see clearly enough to remove the speck from your brother's eye (v. 5). The upshot of this is that sin in our own lives distorts what we see in another's. Moreover, if we take the time to carefully examine our brother's words and actions, and the circumstances that surround him, we are likely to judge him differently than upon first sight. We must judge, but in doing so, we must also keep both of the passages just quoted in view.

But that isn't all. We must judge, but we must also be careful who it is we judge. In Matthew 7, Jesus goes on to warn us that we should not give that which is holy to "dogs" or throw pearls to "pigs." Obviously, in order to obey this command, we must judge people in order to determine who is and who is not a dog or pig. And, in addition, He spends time in the same chapter explaining how we may judge who is a false teacher

(vv. 15–23). Judging, then, is essential. So, you don't tell your judgmental counselee, "Stop judging people."

But before going on, let's see who the dogs and pigs are and what the holy thing and the pearls are. The context about judging continues, with no break in the narrative. We are prohibited from judging dogs and pigs, and warned of the danger of doing so (v. 6). Both are unappreciative of your efforts and the pig may even cause injury. The second part of the verse is reminiscent of Proverbs 9:7, "Whoever reproves a mocker gets insulted, and whoever corrects a wicked person invites bruises." Those words were spoken in somewhat rougher times when people would haul off and hit one another. Today, they will curse you! Don't offer any of your pearls of wisdom to unbelievers in order to correct them; keep from admonishing unbelievers with God's holy truth. Reproof should be for fellow believers since only they can follow it in a way that pleases God (Romans 8:8). That is what He is saying. Paul reiterated the same idea in I Corinthians 5:12–13 when he told us that it isn't the business of believers to go about trying to correct unbelievers. What they need is a presentation of the way of salvation.

As a counselor, you must keep all of these verses in mind when counseling judgmental people. The principles articulated in them are essential to helping them. You must teach them to judgmental people who, for the most part, don't understand them. What they need most is careful exposition and application of Matthew 7, John 7, and I Corinthians 5. Having given it, then move to correctly admonishing and coaching them in the practice of these principles. Take specific instances to work on: judging the boss, your husband, a neighbor, a fellow church member, and so forth. In doing this, you also must heed these verses when judging the words, behavior, and attitudes of your counselees. As Jesus pointed out in Matthew, the sword cuts both ways.

Envious, Jealous, and Bitter

Jealous and bitterly envious persons are not the most pleasant persons to counsel. But, perhaps more frequently than you would like to think, you will meet them in counseling. Indeed, when either of these expressions of nastiness is not present as a principal problem, it is nevertheless possible that it lies just under the surface as a complicating problem.[1] What is the difference between envy and jealousy? Jealousy is an inordinate desire for something that another possesses and you cannot have. A person can be jealous of his neighbor's car, his wife, his job, his house, and so forth. But envy focuses one more on the neighbor than on his car. It is jealousy plus elements of bitterness and resentment.

Psalm 73 in its entirety has to do with these problems. It is the deep resentment and bitterness of the prosperity enjoyed by the wicked that led Asaph to the brink of unbelief. As he said, "My feet almost slipped; my steps nearly went astray for I envied the arrogant; I saw the prosperity of the wicked" (vv. 2, 3, HCSB). He goes on to describe what they have in abundance, how they get away with doing evil, and asks, "Did I purify my heart and wash my hands in innocence for nothing?" (vv. 4–13). He recounts his own afflictions, setting them in contrast to the health and welfare of the wicked. "Is my faith worthwhile, after all?" he began to ask himself. He had a hard time "understanding" this seeming anomaly he confessed. And he came to the point of throwing it all overboard.

But then came resolution. "I entered God's sanctuary. Then I understood their destiny" (v. 17). At this turning point he saw how easily it all could be taken away from them – one category three hurricane and they and their possessions, health, and pride gone, all gone forever! ("Then I understood

---

1. See my *Practical Encyclopedia of Christian Counseling* for information about the difference between principal and complicating problems.

their destiny," v. 17). As this percolated down into his soul, he realized his foolishness because he had forgotten the God he served and had acted like an "unreasoning animal" (v. 22). His thinking and desire had been centered upon the things of this world. He had forgotten God's present guidance by the Word of His "counsel." And the "glory" that would be his at the resurrection (v. 24).

So, pastor, your embittered, envious counselee sits before you asking how it could be that unbelievers seem to be so well off when he has so little. He wants to know why Barry ("that bum") gets the promotion and he is passed by. Barry drinks like a fish, has divorced his wife, and cares nothing for God. Yet he drives a BMW! "How come he has everything and, by comparison, I – who work harder than any two Barrys could – have so little?"

What will you say to him? Nothing.

You may be thinking, "Nothing? What shall I do? I can't just sit there."

Nothing. Don't say a word. Just pick up your Bible and turn to this Psalm. Read it to him – slowly. So he doesn't miss a word. Use a modern translation like the *Holman Christian Standard Bible* that I have been quoting so he won't have any difficulty understanding what you are reading. Here and there, much as I have been doing in this chapter, stop and apply a couple of verses as they apply to him. Then go on reading to the very end. At the conclusion of the reading, ask, "Well, Matt, what have you got to say?"

Should he deny that the Psalm fits his case, ask him, "how come." If he begins to object, "But my situation is different," tell him you can't see how, and ask him to explain why he thinks so. His reply to that one will lead you into your next discussion.

Usually, I suggest quoting only one or two verses in a counseling case, so that you don't "snow" the counselee with Scripture. But in this case, it is precisely a heavy snowfall that is needed! The entire Psalm is so pertinent that he ought to hear it all. Every objection he raises may be countered by one verse or another. If he says, "But I've tried to be a good Christian, and where does it get me?" read verse 13. Then say, "Sounds like your situation to me." If she talks about Kara's prosperity rather than her own, read verse 3 and say, "Again, sounds like you, doesn't it?" If he or she continues in spite of all you have read and said, warn about slipping as Asaph almost did. Reread verse 2 and ask, "Don't you see what your bitter, resentful envy is doing to you?" as you go on to reread verse 21. "Isn't it eating you up inside?" And, you can top it all off by asking whether he prefers the things of this present world more than the glory to come hereafter. At the end of all of this, make it plain that the choice is clear – things or God (vv. 25–28).

Is there anything more to say?

Hasn't God already said it all in Psalm 73?

Wordy

Sure, there's a problem with those who don't know how to speak concisely in counseling. Some talk excessively because they love to hear themselves talk. And, of course, there are those who are repetitious. You will often have to say such things as, "Can you say that once more, simply?" Or, if the problem is repetition, "OK. I got that and wrote it down in my agenda column. We'll get to it in time. Now, for the next matter…" Or, if the speech problem is using psychological, or other types of jargon, explain that your counseling will be done in biblical terms, and you expect him to do likewise.

But what I really want to address is none of the above items. In fact, in this chapter, I'm using the term "wordy" to mean something other than it usually means. You see, I couldn't think of a non–wordy way in which to work "speech" and people" in the title – so I resorted to the misuse of the term "wordy." At any rate, it did provide an opportunity to at least mention those practices in passing.

The old school rhyme that children recited when others called them names was, "Sticks and stones may break my bones, but words can never hurt me." How false that is! In Proverbs 18:6, God says, "A stubborn fool's lips cause contention." You've known situations in which unnecessary controversy takes place because someone spoke foolishly, I am certain. Proverbs 12:6 declares "The words of the wicked are a bloody ambush." Such words show how serious hurtful talk can be; lives may even be at stake as the result of harmful speech. Speech and violence are often connected. Many words, though not physically injurious, may cut to the inner core of another. Listen to this: "There is a kind of careless speaking that is like sword thrusts" (Proverbs 12:18). To top it off, here this: "Death and life are in the tongue" (Proverbs 18:21).

"Words can never hurt me?" Wrong. Not only can speech cut and slash others, the speaker's words may be self-destructive: "He who opens wide his lips, ruins himself" (Proverbs 13:3b). We read, "A gossip separates friends" (Proverbs 16:28). We read, "The mouth of the wicked pours forth evil things" (Proverbs 15:28). Of course, such evil may be vile, blasphemous, filthy or otherwise. But it may also be evil in that it will tear down another's reputation. Gossip, which I just mentioned, has not only separated friends elsewhere, but also members of Christ's church. Gossip is spreading information (true or false) to persons who have no right to it. It is a violation of many passages that forbid talking negatively about another behind his back.

People with caustic speech, careless speech, and hypocritical speech and the like are mentioned again in the Proverbs. From the sheer volume of entries about speech in this one book of the Bible you can readily understand the prominence which God gives to the matter. What must you do with such counselees? First, reprove them. Second, show from these verses and others how strongly God objects to such communication on their part. Thirdly, turn to the many passages in Proverbs that show how beneficial the right kind of speech can be and develop homework assignments calculated to help your counselees learn how to begin to help rather than hurt others through speech. Here is a list of verses that you might want to use:

> Life flows from righteous speech. Proverbs 10:11
>
> Wisdom can be shared by means of speech that is acceptable to God. Proverbs 10:31, 32
>
> By sharing knowledge of the truth it is possible to help one's friend. Proverbs 11:9
>
> By counsel and helpful speech those who hurt can be healed. Proverbs 12:18
>
> Many earn their living by speech (e.g., preachers). Proverbs 13:2

Speech can bring joy to others.   Proverbs 15:23

Now, these are but samples, once more from but a part of Proverbs of how helpful speech can be. You can look up the number of other entries that are to be found in this book and other books of the Bible. But there is one more passage of significance that you should have at hand when dealing with counselees who have problems handling their speech in constructive ways. It is Ephesians 4:29–32. I shall not quote it, but I want to point out a couple of things you might look for when reading it for yourself. First, note how strongly God speaks through the apostle Paul. In verse 29, the word describing wrong word is literally, "putrid." Notice, also, the frightening and sobering effect of hurtful words that don't build others up, but tear them down. He says in verse 30 that such words *grieve* God's Holy Spirit. This anthropomorphism is a very strong and moving one. What Paul is saying is that if God, the Spirit, were a man, when He heard such rotten words, He would feel pained by the curse, a Spirit cannot truly be pained because He has no body. Nevertheless, whatever in God would be comparable to human pain is the result of hearing Christians using words that destroy their brothers. That, I say, is a sobering thought. Don't be hesitant to explain them to your counselees. The apostle wasn't hesitant to express himself this way to the Ephesians. In conclusion, let me urge you to deal with the speech of others to help them to learn to speak in an edifying manner.

Overly Casual

It's not that they're necessarily indifferent (they just don't get excited about anything). They probably want to do the right thing, in many cases, but you'd never know it unless you had first unearthed it, by a lot of digging.

You say to a counselee, "So, you see what God wants you to do?" The response: "Yeah. By the way, did you see the game last night?" You answer, "No. Why do you ask? Did something take place that's pertinent to this homework assignment?" Response: "I don't think so."

— Well, then, Brad, why did you bring it up?

— Oh, I don't know. Just happened to think of it.

— I see. Well, let's get back to work.

— Sure, why not?

— Do you understand the assignment. And are you committed to doing what you agreed to do?

— Can't see any reason why I can't.

— Does that mean "Yes"?

— Yep.

— Is there anything else I should know before we close this session

— Oh. I probably should mention that my wife's been talking divorce again.

— Again? You never told me anything about this before. And you didn't put it on your PDI that she *ever* did. Why not?

— Didn't think it was all that important. Came to talk about the job problem I'm having. She doesn't mean anything by it. I'm not concerned.

— Not important? You're not concerned? You should be! We need to get her in here as soon as possible. I don't think that we should even wait until the next session. You could call her now and see if she can come with you tomorrow evening. Agreed?

— Sure. Nothing to get excited about though. But who knows, it might do some good for both of us to see you together.

— Do you ever get excited about anything, Brad?

— Can't think of anything right now.

— Here's the phone.

Christians like Brad need to have their faith stirred up. The Bible describes the Christian life as vibrant, even exciting. Jesus described it as living life "abundantly" (John 10:10). Christians, who live that way, are enthusiastic people. When a believer becomes enthusiastic for God, that enthusiasm spills over into all of his life. Read these words to your apathetic counselee, "Zeal for your house will eat Me up" (John 2:17), and then say something like this, "Now, that's enthusiasm for you! The passage describes the Lord Jesus Christ. Zeal is excessive enthusiasm – more than one usually shows. Because of it, He carried out the cleansing of the temple in such a way that others dared not stop Him! We're going to aim for zeal like that, but we'll begin with simple enthusiasm."

Now, a person who is overly casual isn't likely to be a Bible student. And he certainly isn't enjoying abundant life. That's probably a major reason for his overly-casual attitude. You will need to get him into the habit of studying God's Word in ways that affect his life. Perhaps you could show him what enthusiasm for Scripture is like by reading some of Psalm 119. It is the record of a man who lived day by day with his Bible. Enthusiasm – even in the midst of life's vicissitudes – runs throughout the Psalm. Read also a couple of other Psalms (try Psalm 145, 146, or 147) and show him what real enthusiasm looks like.

Brad, and others like him, need to learn to be up front about their problems. They seem to be trying to pass off anything that they can't deal with as unimportant. Assumed casualness, which can become a way of life, is their preferred method for doing so. A combination of facing life squarely and learning enthusiasm for the Lord, Who will assist in doing so as His Word is applied, is exactly what they need.

Somewhere along the line, you might want to show how repulsive your counselee's attitude is to God. Read Revelation 3:15, 16 to him. If he isn't already being chastised for his lukewarmness by difficulties that have come his way, warn him that chastening will come if he doesn't change. Tell him it's time to get a life – God's kind!

Upon repentance, he should then be enlisted in some service for the Lord. Nothing creates more enthusiasm than working with other Christians who are also faithfully serving Christ. Chances are, he has never been involved in anything of the sort.

Being "cool" in the face of trial is one thing; *playing it cool* is another. Help such brothers and sisters; they are probably hurting beneath their skins (and hurting others by their attitudes).

Hasty

The old saying, "Haste makes waste," is certainly true. Doubtless, it was obvious enough for someone to devise the proverb. When a person hurries to accomplish something without proper preparation, tries to do it without the necessary tools, or spills, drops or smashes it because he doesn't take time to do it well, there is "waste." But it isn't only waste that occurs from haste. God tells us in His own proverb concerning haste, "Also, it isn't good for a person to be without knowledge; and he who rushes with his feet sins." Haste makes waste – but it also makes *sin*.

In a counselor, haste without knowledge of his counselee's problems may cause him to sin against him. How? Those, for instance, who think that one solution fits all counselees (e.g., Charles Solomon) and fail to gather adequate data about the counselee are an example of such haste. Haste on the part of Job's counselors, who did not bother to gather facts because they had made up their minds, caused him much suffering on top of the pain that he was enduring. And even when he explained his situation to them they refused to listen to him.

But counselees, in particular, who try to anticipate where your counseling will go next before actually finding out what you plan for them to do, may botch up a good biblical plan of action by their haste.

Those who achieve in various activities, when they have acquired neither the knowledge nor the skills to achieve in another field are another case in point. We've all seen the commercials where football players advertise shaving equipment. What I'm talking about is along the same lines. People are foolish to be persuaded by such advertisements. Counselees are equally foolish when they thus persuade themselves!

How often a business has failed because someone went into it with good ideas but insufficient capital! Desire to "get rich quick" is one sample of this. People who fall for the ads telling them that they can make a bundle by using their phone for three hours a day at home are another example. Consider Proverbs 21:5: "Plans of the diligent lead only to plenty, but those of every hasty person lead only to poverty!" They want lots of money quickly, without putting much into the business – either of capital or effort. The classic passage in I Timothy 6:9ff about those who make riches their goal may be used powerfully when dealing with counselees like this. Moreover, this from Proverbs is pertinent: "A stingy man is in a hurry to acquire wealth, but he doesn't know that poverty will overtake him" (Proverbs 28:22). Because he won't invest enough of himself or his money in the effort he fails. Or, having begun a business, he won't invest enough capital to assure excellence, the product that he produces is inferior, and people, having used it once, have no desire to purchase it again. You will counsel people who may not have businesses, but who because of stinginess are in a hurry – and fail!

But it isn't only wealth that we should consider. Trouble of all sorts comes to those who don't take the time to consider their ways. Proverbs 14:16 says, "The wise person fears and avoids evil [trouble[1]], but the stupid fool passes on and is reckless." A parent who has a two-year-old that "gets into everything," is a "fool" if he leaves sharp objects or pills lying around where the child can get hold of them. He should beforehand "fear" trouble and thus avoid it. The one who fails to think ahead about such matters is reckless and his child may end up with a serious injury. He's in a hurry to do what he wants to do, so he fails to take time to use precautionary measures. The one who drives too fast because he is in a hurry to get somewhere, drives "recklessly." He places himself and others at risk. He may run red lights and smash into another car, causing trouble (and possible injury) to all involved in the accident.

---

1. The word "evil" is used in Scripture two ways: 1) the evil one commits; 2) the evil or troubles that he endures.

Much haste is the result of poor planning. This usually involves a failure to schedule one's time well (or even to schedule it at all). You will often find it necessary to help counselees organize their time. You will find that the shoddy homework that some counselees do is the result of waiting until the last minute to do it – all because of failure to schedule it and follow the schedule. Hurried homework is usually wasted homework. So, you must teach counselees how to schedule and coach them in following schedules once they have begun to set them up.

Inferior work comes not merely from haste in gaining wealth, but from haste in doing something unpleasant. To avoid as little unpleasantness as possible, he hurries to "get it over with." Many tasks (especially counseling homework) are unpleasant. The tendency, when fulfilling them, therefore, is to finish as soon as possible. Counselees who do homework assignments carelessly probably do other things that way as well, thus causing much unnecessary complications to their other difficulties. Keep an eye open for this dynamic and probe to see if reckless activity, due to haste, may be what is keeping your counselee from truly advancing at a more rapid pace. It's enigmatic, but true, that in a hurry to do things that take time, one wastes time and ends up taking longer than he has to. You will often have to help people who are embedded in such patterns of hasty action to get out of them. Doing so begins with helping them to recognize that haste – when not called for – is sin. The hasty counselee runs many risks, most of which are minor (and, therefore, don't cause enough personal trouble to make him abandon the practice of acting hastily), but if it becomes a way of life sooner or later he will fall into more serious ones. Indeed, he may be sitting right there before you in your counseling office because he did so!

Self-Assured

The self-assured person dwells next door to the hasty one. How is that? Because the hasty person "hasn't time" to do a task the right way, but does a "rush job" in order to get it over with. The self-assured person thinks that because he's generally capable in other areas he doesn't need to take the time others normally do to learn or accomplish some work. So, unprepared (or in an unskilled manner), he or she ploughs ahead making uneven rows. He ruins things all the time.

Some self-assured women, for instance, don't bother to learn how to cook well. They know that they did well in school and in other activities of life, so, "of course" they can cook as well! "Anyone can do that; there's nothing to it." Oh? Well, why were those biscuits as hard as a rock? Why did that last cake fell apart? How is it that the coffee tastes like dishwater, the steaks like leather, and the toast is burned to a crisp? Those are the thoughts (if not spoken words) of the longsuffering husbands of self-assured women.

"You don't need to teach me how to do it." That's a sentiment common to the self-assured. "Sure, I can do it," is another. How about this for a third: "Just leave it to me." One more? Sure. Here it is: "Consider it done."

In all of this over-confidence in oneself there is a large element of pride. You will hear it in the criticisms that the self-assured often level at others. But the Scriptures put the finger on the source of failure this way: "Before honor is humility" (Proverbs 15:33). The self-assured person lacks humility. Whether it's the honor her husband shows by the satisfying sounds he emits at the dinner table, or the honor bestowed on the winner of a marathon, it doesn't matter. The principle is always the same: one must learn the knowledge and skills necessary in order to accomplish a task in an honorable manner. But to learn, he or she must be humble. One must admit that he doesn't have the knowledge and skills that he doesn't have!

I have known young men studying for the ministry that want to tell their professors what to teach. These are the ones who barely get by in order to graduate because "to really study that stuff is a waste of time." Then, when they get out into the pastorate, after a year or so, and the congregation dwindles away to practically nothing, they can't bring themselves to ask the help of an older minister concerning their grammar, their exegesis, and the preparation of sermons. They stumble through several churches and end up selling real estate.

Self-assured people lack the very quality that they seek: honor. Earlier, I quoted half of Proverbs 15:33, "Before honor is humility." Consider also the other half: "The fear of Yahweh is wise discipline." The term "fear of Yahweh" is a technical term in the Scriptures that means "a life that is faithfully lived before God." Such a life, lived in His presence, is always a "disciplined" one. To wisely discipline oneself to live in ways that please God is, as we saw, to humbly take advantage of every opportunity to learn. And the one thing necessary to humble learning is discipline.

Discipline doesn't come easily. That's what the self-assured person has not realized. He thinks that he can do things without going through the ropes, without the rigors of training. But discipline requires hard work, regularity and consistency. And like the hasty person, who doesn't have time to do things well, the self-assured person is a close neighbor since he won't put out the effort to learn.

In the next chapter we will visit next door – the neighbor who lives on the other side of the self-assured person. Actually, the three neighbors keep close company with one another and, though differing in the reasons for their lack of disciplined work, need much the same encouragement. Having repented of their sinful ways, they need to humbly learn to do things that please God in ways that please Him, by putting in the hard work that this requires.

Glib

He may make it for a short time, but in the ministry the preacher who attempts to get by without study and effort to prepare his sermons as he ought, will soon be found out by his congregation. Glib preachers, all sound and no substance (along with many congressmen), perhaps best personify the type. The salesman, hawking some inferior product as the best of the line, the young man sweet-talking the girl he plans to seduce, and the boaster who talks a good game, are all varieties of the glib person. They run each other a close race!

The trouble with these deceivers (and that's exactly what they are) is that there is nothing to back up what they say. They are "all sound and fury, signifying nothing," as Shakespeare put it. They are all talk with no substance.

If you're not careful and alert when counseling them, they will spin a tale with such a straight face that you'll believe it. They are, to one extent or another, "confidence men." They use their verbal nostrums and snake oils to deceive you and others (and often themselves as well). They are verbal shysters and rhetorical quacks who hustle their wares to unsuspecting and naïve persons. But as a counselor, one of the last things that you must be is naïve.

Of course, as a biblical counselor, who believes that works should follow faith, you have a way to find them out – homework! Because they don't (or can't) do it, they will thereby tip their hands. You will have your hands full in attempting to bring them to repentance. They can spin a plausible yarn or two for why you should surely excuse and certainly not accuse them. They will say, "You see, it's this way..." or, "To tell the truth..." Look out for such expressions. Why should anyone have to add, "to tell the truth" to his statements? If his yea is yea and his nay is nay, there is no need for such assurances. His word itself should be trustworthy. The only reason for the unnecessary addition is that he is not doing what he says – he usually isn't telling the truth! Watch out for this: by their language you will know them. When you hear such remarks, double check everything he says.

Glib people want to "make it" with their mouths. But when they are found out, often enough people stop believing anything they say, and their ploys cease to work for them. It is then that they end up on your doorstep, wondering why they failed. It will be your task to encourage them to recognize the fact that they have been trying to substitute talk for toil. They will have to change their lifestyle completely, so that they "make it" by the fruit of the Spirit which comes when one endeavors by His help to do what the Scriptures require of him. Philippians 2:13 will probably come into your discussion at one point or another.

The apostle Paul wasn't as eloquent as Apollos, it seems, but the latter, though eloquent, couldn't make it by that alone. He needed the instruction that Prisca and Aquila gave him. He was humble enough to receive their help – even though he was already known for his eloquence.

Because he has learned to get along until now by glibness, in deceiving others he may have also deceived himself. Self-deception, when recognized in oneself, often takes its toll on the deceiver. He has learned to believe his own tales (at least to some extent). When recognized, the awakening may be like the brilliance of a new morning flooding in so that he must rub his eyes in order to shake off the dark remnants of his past life. The sunlight will reveal the self-deception; you must lead him by the hand into the new pathway of truth. It will not come all at once, he will try over and over again to deceive you (wittingly or otherwise), but when he does so you must astutely recognize what is happening and once more bring the fact to light. Glib persons are sad persons when everything falls apart and fragile in the aftermath. Give them care. They need it!

Vivacious

If nothing else, they will tire you out! In contrast to your overly-casual counselees, you will also encounter those whose enthusiasm overwhelms their judgment. Without full understanding, which they won't take the time to acquire, they plunge ahead anxious to "get at it" (usually it doesn't matter what the "it" is so long as they see it as a goal to be reached). Indeed, the "it" is likely to be vague or even not more than a rough outline, but they are ready to set out to accomplish it – today!

You will probably have trouble reining them in. Like a horse that jumps the gun, they race forward as soon as you give them the slightest idea of where counseling may be heading. They see the goal, are anxious to cross the finish line, but forget to plan for the laps that lay between. As a consequence, their desire to "get it done" causes them to neglect the essentials needed to reach the finish line.

— You need to straighten things out with Jennifer, Barb. Now, here's how to...

— Right! I can't wait to do it. I know it's the proper thing to do. It's on my "to do" list for tomorrow morning. I'll call her right away. Anything more I need to do this week?

— Well, as I was about to say, Barb, when you visit with Jennifer, you will want to...

— No need to convince me further, pastor. I know you're right and I'm committed to doing everything possible to solve the problem. Don't think I'll shirk my responsibility.

And so it goes. You'll do well to get a word in "sledgewise"!

When the Barbs of this world set their minds on something you can be certain that if it's humanly possible, they will do it. Of that you can be sure. But they will do it without giving previous thought to how to go about it. You will want to discuss with them the right approach – that they confess their sin so that they won't do more harm than good. But they're already oriented toward the next homework assignment before you can begin. You will have to slow them down, explain that it's not a matter of going and doing, but of going at the right way, in the right time, and doing what must be done well. Details often elude the vivacious type.

At times, such people will need little instruction if there is no danger of messing things up. When that's so, OK. But be certain that they don't convince you that this is the case when, in fact, it isn't. And don't let their eagerness to accomplish something keep you from taking the time to discuss the ways and means of doing it. Their enthusiasm can be disarming. But just as the glib person who attempts to get along with talk alone, the vivacious person is likely to think that enthusiasm is all that she needs. Usually, that isn't so. Then, when things turn out poorly, she will wonder, "Was the reason bad counsel, or was Jennifer at fault, or..."

You must be careful not to smother vivacity, however. Instead, capitalize on this lively enthusiasm! Rather than dampen enthusiasm, commend them for it, but insist on them taking time to prepare well for whatever tasks they undertake. Warn them that zeal without knowledge usually does damage.

What a Barb like this needs is direction. If she blunders ahead, understanding neither the dangers nor the intricacies of confession and forgiveness, she may end up widening the gap between herself and her estranged friend. It's possible that it was Barb's undirected zeal that caused the rupture between them in the first place. So *slow her down*. Pull in the reins and stop the Barbs you counsel from recklessly dashing into trouble.

Vivacity is liveliness – a quality to be desired in a counselee. But some vivacious persons will neglect attending to important details. Often, they don't take time to think of anything but the big picture. They probably aren't bean counters to begin with. And, when they fail, they think that what they must do to rectify matters is to put more energy into the enterprise. That, of course, is precisely what they must not do! More energy, wrongly channeled and directed, will only aggravate the situation.

When I think of such people, what comes to mind is someone in the deep end of the pool who doesn't know how to swim, thinking that the more energy he exerts flailing his arms and legs about, the better off he will be. But flailing about isn't swimming. What is lacking isn't energy but knowledge and skill. What he needs at the moment isn't energy, but a lifeguard! That's your role counselor. Then, having rescued him from drowning, your role changes to that of a swimming instructor.

Thank God when you come across a vivacious person. Such people, properly directed, will get things done. Paul set as his goal for the churches scattered around the island of Crete the goal of doing good works (Titus 2:14). But as in the lives of those new believers in Crete, so your vivacious person will need instruction about how to achieve the goal. Paul left Titus behind to get them organized and instructed. Young converts, today, may tend to be overly anxious to do things for the Lord. That's great. But they, too, need direction. Don't throw cold water on their enthusiasm – curb it and direct it. New, vivacious converts can be a vital asset to any congregation.

Vacillators

These persons need to learn to look neither to the left nor to the right, but straight ahead. Like horses that tend to be distracted, they need to be fitted with biblical blinders. Today it's this, tomorrow it's that. Never a session goes by but some new suggestion is made, some new problem is raised, some new distraction arises. You task, difficult as it may be at times, will be to keep your counselee from deviating from the issue at hand or the task God wants him to perform. You must learn to keep vacillating persons on track.

Elijah had to face the problem, as it manifested itself in one form. He found it necessary to challenge vacillating Israelites to make a decision to serve either Yahweh or Baal. It is especially interesting to note the description that he gave of the people when making the challenge. Referring to a lame man who totters along, swaying to the right then to the left, he asked them, "Why do you sway between two opinions?" (I Kings 18:21, translation is mine). He called for decisive action. Their "hesitation" (HCSB) was displeasing to God. He insisted on them deciding who is the true God, and, then, to serve Him. When it comes to matters of serving and pleasing God – as most matters in counseling are – indecision must be condemned. Counselees must make up their minds to do God's will and then do it, and stick to doing it.

Just as your counselee decided once to place his trust in Jesus Christ as Savior, so too, he must decide to do all that Jesus commanded (Matthew 28:20). Just as there could be no swaying back and forth about salvation, so too there can be no leaning to one side and then to the other about obeying counseling assignments that are clearly based upon God's authoritative Word.

— Carl, you simply must break that sinful relationship. There is no biblical justification for living together with her out of wedlock.

— I know, pastor, but...

— How can there be any "but" about it? God's Word is clear.

— I know. But what's going to happen to Lacy?

— That is a separate issue. It can be decided only after you move out of her apartment.

— I know I should do the right thing...but...

— Do you dare to say "but" to God? He won't accept your excuses. You're not telling me "but," you're saying "no" to God. That's serious business.

— Yesterday I wanted to, but today...

Having finally said about all you can say, like Elijah did, you must call upon him to stop vacillating and (to bring the metaphor up to date) bite the bullet: "You see, God knew we'd tend to deviate from His way. So He plainly warned against it in Proverbs 4:25–27, when He said, in effect, Keep your eyes fixed on the goal straight ahead of you. Don't let anything or anyone persuade you to deviate from it. He knew that there would be more than enough other ways that appealed to the habits of sin that still affect us. So He warned us. Now, Carl, this isn't even an iffy question. God has already made the decision for you: fornication is a sin that He will not countenance in His children. You must hesitate no longer. Repent, and give it up – once for all!"

James called hesitation of this sort "double-mindedness" (James 1:6–8). He described vacillating persons like Carl as "waves," driven in whatever direction the wind may blow (v. 6). He further pointed out that those who are double-minded about obeying God become unstable (undependable) in "all their ways" (v. 8). And, to boot, God said that he will not answer the prayers of those who vacillate (v. 7). That places Carl, and those like him, in a precarious position – the double-minded man's communication with God has been cut off! To become unreliable in all areas of life is precisely what happens to the vacillating Christian. He is undependable at church when you ask him to do something. Friends can't be sure he will come through for them. His family knows not to trust any responsibility to him. To put it simply, he makes a mess of his life!

Instead, James wanted his readers to become people who "have it all together." That is precisely what the word he uses in verse 1:4 means. He is to be "complete," as some versions have it, "integrated," as we might as easily translate it. James is speaking of stable persons, those upon whom you can depend. When they tell you they are going to do something, they do it. When they make a promise they keep it. They don't vacillate about such things.

The integrated person that James wrote about is one whose life revolves around a magnetic center. That magnet is God. It powerfully attracts every aspect of his life to Him. As these are pulled together, he becomes the *teleios* ("integrated") person James describes. If there is any aspect of his person that lacks integration – doesn't move toward that center – James says ask God for that which is lacking (v. 5). And, though possibly cut off from communication about other matters, that is one prayer He will answer. If he is sincere about wanting to become an integrated person, God can make him such (v. 5). Because of the vital importance of the matter, the vacillating person must be helped. Don't neglect him simply because he is irritating. You can expect that. Just stand firm and give him the help he needs.

The person I'm describing isn't the one who can't decide because the evidence is so slim. Rather, he is the one who, in the face of the facts, still finds it difficult to take the biblical course of action. He fears (or at least wonders about) the consequences. He may be hovering between obedience to God and avoiding an unpleasant obligation. In one session he seems to have settled the matter; in the next he isn't so sure. This hesitation can go on indefinitely unless, like Elijah, you call a halt to it. You dare not allow it to continue if you are going to help him. If no change is forthcoming, you may have to threaten the use of church discipline to bring about a definite change in his life. Naturally, you will reserve discipline as a final resort. But you may have to threaten it sooner, rather then later.

Polite

"Isn't politeness a good thing?" Of course it is; modern American society could use a heap more of it! But politeness can become an excuse for inaction and for failure to tell the truth. When I moved to the South, one of the more pleasant surprises was to realize that I had entered a more polite society. To find helpful and kind people who would go out of their way to assist you was a definite boon. It isn't all outward show, as many Northerners suppose; it's genuine.

In spite of this, although in no way do I want to demean those who exhibit this pleasant sort of politeness with all of its good results, there is a sort of politeness that can also become a detriment to counseling. And you must become aware of it. When it is necessary to tell the unvarnished truth, or to take some disciplinary action against an unrepentant brother or sister at church, politeness can get in the way. "I could never do that; it's against my upbringing," is what one may say (or think). Now, I don't want anyone to think that being polite is wrong; but it can become a hindrance when it gets in the way of following Scripture. The response, of course, may be nothing more than an insincere excuse, though often it is not. There are people who are genuinely horrified at the thought of confronting another to help him get out of his sin as God, in Galatians 6:1, commands.[1] Tell someone like this that God requires it, and it is likely that he will balk. The Northerner might also balk. But the reasons in each case will be different. In spite of the cordiality that is shown to one another in such places as the South and much of the Midwest, it must not be allowed to get in the way of truth and obedience. You must confront it. Contextualization can go too far!

---

1. For details, see my book on Galatians 6:1ff called *Ready to Restore*.

No, I'm not speaking about becoming gruff or impolite. One need not use anything but polite language. Politely saying hard things, while not shading the truth, is essential. It is as necessary for a counselor as it is for the physician who must deliver bad news; but when it is the right thing to do, it must be done. If you are a counselor who has problems with this, you must learn to "speak the truth in love" (Ephesians 4:15). It can be done, politely, constructively (see also Ephesians 4:29–32).

There is often a fine line between what a person takes offense at and what is truly offensive. Moreover, many today in politically correct circles take offense at the strangest things. Many were upset about calling a team the "Braves," even though it was a complimentary term that the American Indians didn't seem to mind at all. The feminization of language is another current fad. The idea is to omit the universal or generalizing use of the masculine pronoun "he." This leads to an ear-hurting misuse of grammar (but if anyone cares, *they* can go ahead and do it anyway). And, not to be omitted, is the disgusting practice of some modern commentaries to speak of the "Son of humanity" rather than the "Son of man."

It is not your task, counselor, to cater to the whims of the PC people and other liberals, or even to the picky prejudices of some counselees. To bind your conscience by their preferences is wrong when it means failure to speak the truth. So, when dealing with "politeness," be sure to be no more or no less polite than the Scriptures, rightly interpreted. Politeness, in the long run, is to do God's will God's way.

Bored

Life is only boring to those who make it so. There are so many exciting things to experience in God's world that there is never a good reason to be bored. The creation itself is fascinating. Activities of all sorts can be all-engrossing. Other people can be interesting. If nothing else, to the believer, the study of the Scriptures should be compelling. If the Bible doesn't interest (or even bores) your counselee, clearly he has a problem that must be dealt with.

When one acts bored, or says he is, ask him, "Is there nothing that is of vital interest to you?" His response will probably provide the information you need to know in order to help him. Suppose he answers, "I'm bored with everything" or "I'm bored with life in general." If, indeed, he means it, you know that his problem is serious. His entire life has become a hopeless succession of uninviting chores. Naturally, it did not become this way on its own. In one way or another; your counselee brought it on himself. He is looking at life through homemade eyeglasses. He has determined that because many aspects of life are unpleasant, and others hold no interest for him, that he might as well give up on life in general. The fact is, given the desire to do so, almost anything can be made interesting.

One reason people are bored is because in this age of TV and other electronic devices, counselees no longer know how to entertain themselves. They must *be* entertained. Even children, nurtured on the milk of TV and computer-generated games, find themselves bored when these devices are not available. This lack of ability to find ways of doing interesting and worthwhile things can carry over into adult life.

Bored people are usually boring people. They are often dull, uninteresting, listless, and drab in their outlook, speech, and composure. Consequently, others avoid them. They invite this by their self-focused, dissatisfied outlook on things. Ask a counselee like this any question and his answer is likely to be "Oh, I don't know." Or, if he responds in any detail, his response will be in tones of gray.

What's wrong with these counselees? Fundamentally, they lack a sense of the importance of God's ways. People who are caught up in the utter cruciality of Christianity are not bored. They truly understand that God is behind all that happens both as the Planner of all events and the providential executor of them and are not bored. They are entranced with His ways and His works. They cannot get enough knowledge of them. While they cannot now comprehend why all things happen as they do, nevertheless, they believe that God works in all things for the good of His people. History, which they recognize as His story, for them is anything but boring. They watch as it unfolds, entranced, waiting to see what God will do next.

Their lives are not boring because they know that they are members of God's family. Life isn't dependent on things, sports, or other artificial entertainments. They find joy in fellowshipping with other members of the Father's family. They are excited to be part of the greatest cause there is – the spreading of God's truth to the nations. They are a part of a band of praying persons who have Someone to talk to when there is no one else around. Day or night, they have Someone to talk to about anything that is on their hearts – and, like many who are uninterested, He listens! They are looking forward to a blessed future with Him and the rest of the family, gathered in a place where righteousness is at home. There will be no failure, frailty, or frustration – only a future filled with holy fun and frolic.

When tempted to be bored by a society around them that is bored with one another, they turn to the study of the Scriptures where, to eyes that can see and hearts that believe, they may revel in the truth they are privileged to read. Nothing can set their hearts aflame like discovering and discussing truths that they have just uncovered in the pages of the Book! The freshness of biblical insights into the mind of God and

His ways with His world is a unique pleasure enjoyed by faithful Christians. Others know nothing of it.

Your opportunity, counselor, is to so excite your believing counselees about learning more truth from the Bible that they will never again have cause to be bored. Help them to learn how to study rather than merely read the Bible. Pastors should provide such instruction to enable Christians to do it. Mere reading, without understanding, can become boring. Those who are guided by the pages of divine revelation not only find that their lives take on a new meaning, but the radiance of their new way of life can be noticeable to others as well. Consequently, people genuinely excited about Jesus Christ as He is set forth in the Scriptures, can be neither bored nor boring.

Idiosyncratic

Some people are different. They "do their own thing." When I say "different," I mean *very* different! Some people call them "strange" or "weirdos." The Scriptures call them "eccentric" (*atopos* = "out of place," literally, or in the present day vernacular, "out of it"). When we say, "He's out of it," we mean that he just doesn't seem to get it – whatever the "it" may be. Other current terms that express a similar thought are "spacey" and "airhead." *Atopos* people seem to be always in their own little realm, often oblivious of what's going on around them or how they are affecting others. As the word, *atopos* indicates, they aren't "with it," they're "out of place," seemingly somewhere else in their thoughts.

Paul warned against such people in II Thessalonians 3:2. In that verse, he was speaking of unbelievers, but the description also fits believers who have carried over their old life patterns into the new life. Evidently, by their unusual behavior, they had been upsetting churches. Certainly, over the years, I must admit that our Bible believing churches have attracted their fair share of them. It isn't because the message that we teach is so strange that they want to become a part of our congregations, but probably because conservative, Christian churches have been willing to put up with their antics.

Now, from what I am saying, I hope you will understand that I'm not talking about the peculiar ways that each one of us has. They are problem enough! What Paul meant was people who are, as they say, "way out." These are the people who, when talking to you may practically touch noses with you. They are people that hang around listening to private conversations. They come up to visitors and say peculiar things. They hang on to members of the congregation when it is inappropriate to do so.

In counseling, they have a hard time understanding what you tell them – or worse – they will misunderstand and go off and do something entirely different from what you intended. To assure yourselves that they *do* understand, you must pay special attention to explanations and to homework assignments that you give them. That means going over explanations and assignments again and again, having the counselee repeat in his own words what you said, and making sure that your written assignments are clear, uncomplicated, and brief.

It isn't pleasant to have people in the church who blurt out strange things in conversations, who may go up to strangers and greet them in peculiar ways, and in general, make it difficult for others to know how to respond to what they say. Such people need much help in reorienting their lives. Often, this will involve, first, getting them to recognize their peculiarities. Then, it will require bringing them to the place where they are willing to make changes. Finally, it may mean assigning someone in the church to spend time with them instructing them in ways that are more congenial to Christian fellowship.

People fall into such patterns of living for various reasons. Perhaps, one has been a loner all his or her life. He may have grown up in a family where he had to fend for himself. He may have never learned the niceties of interpersonal relationships. He may have been saved off the street and still carries much baggage from his former life with him. Many other past experiences may account for *atopos* behavior. But it isn't our basic concern to delve into these. What we must consider is what strange ways hurt his testimony for Christ, alienate others, and give the Lord and His church a bad name before the world. Those ought to be of prime interest. As we are able to acclimate him into the fellowship of other Christians who are *topos* (literally, "there," or "with it") we want to see him become a valuable member of the congregation so that the gifts that God has given him may be of benefit to the whole body of believers.

Small-Souled

What on earth is a small-souled individual? It is a type of person that Paul said we would confront and need to encourage. The expression is found in I Thessalonians 5:14: "counsel the idle, encourage the timid (literally "small-souled"), support the weak, be patient with everyone." These people, according to the Apostle, need "encouragement" (*parakaleo*). This word for encouragement is a large one. It means to come and help those who need it. It can be translated lawyer, counselor, or merely one who helps in whatever way one needs it. Probably the very best way to think about it is to translate it "help." The type of help needed is defined in each instance by the context, by what it is that a person needs by way of help.

So what sort of help do the "small-souled" need? Clearly, they need expansion of their souls. They do not need coddling. But the need to be encouraged (helped) to grow larger souls. Picture, if you will, people with little, shriveled-up souls. There isn't much going on in their interior life. They do not experience the potential that they have as a child of God. Rather, they neglect it, don't know how to grow their souls, or otherwise are caught in the trap of living very shallow, small lives. They don't use the gifts that God has apportioned them, they are content (or miserable, as the case may be) with their truncated existence, but they lack the spiritual gumption to do anything about it. Indeed, in most cases, they may not know how to do so. They need your help desperately to escape from smallness of soul into a flourishing, growing existence.

How will you encourage them? First, check out to see if they have the courage to step out with those weak souls into new exploits for Christ. If you can't discover something that they have always wanted to do, but didn't have the courage or get-up-and-go to begin it, they'll probably never progress. If it is something that seems feasible for them, lay out a sequence of events that will lead to the goal. In other words,

85

capitalize on their biblically legitimate desires and help them to reach them. They will, of course, need more than a plan (though this will be essential so they can see how it is possible to reach their goals). They will need heavy couching all along the way. You cannot do this in a couple of weeks. It will take longer. You must commit yourself to spending the time and energy to encourage when there is failure, when there are questions about the possibility to do so, etc. You must be on hand to help in responding to them, all the while exuding hope.

Then, there are those who are so shriveled up that they have no desires. They have settled for the status quo. It may not be pleasant, but they have no expectation of doing anything more than they are at present. They must be encouraged to think differently. The idea that God has gifted all of his children for the benefit of the entire body of Christians should be emphasized and fully explained. Then, an examination of his gifts as they have been manifested – even in ever so small ways – should be pursued. Hitting upon possibilities, again a plan and much hopeful encouragement (as well as some pushing and pulling) may be necessary to get the project off the ground. The main thing is to keep the goal in sight. Begin with small goals in the direction of gift use. For example, maybe he has some experience with lawn care – perhaps the only thing that he does for recreation is plant and care for flowers. Well, take it from there! Can you set him up to provide flowers for the table before the pulpit now and then, for special occasions, and for the sick. This last idea may be all that you can begin with, but it will get him in touch with others rather than living by himself, inside of himself.

The small-souled may resist, protesting that they just can't do what you are suggesting. If so, don't accept this excuse (I'm assuming that the suggested work is feasible for them), but you shouldn't take "no" for an answer. Turn to I Corinthians 10:13, hand him a copy of *Christ and your Problems*, and have him report next session about whether or not he still believes the same way about the plan you have sketched out. Then, take it from there. These people are surely in need of help; see that they don't continue without it.

Contentious

Everything that is said or done becomes an issue – something to argue about. It begins when Marty and Kathy come into the room. He takes a seat and she comments, "Well, you might have pulled up my chair for me." He responds, "There you go even before we have a chance to talk to the counselor." She humphs, and turns her head away from him in a defiant manner. You begin to discuss their PDIs, which are full of accusations about one another. You start by reading her comments on the last page about what the problem is. Before you can say anything more, she asks, "Why didn't you read his first? Are you men ganging up on me?"

This is the way it begins. If you allow it to continue, there will be no effective counseling. As soon as you recognize what is happening you must bring it to a halt. Say something like this: "If you continue to argue, we'll get nowhere. From now on, I want you to address me if you have something to say, and not to speak negatively to one another. OK." If they argue about this restriction, then you need to make it absolutely clear that you will not counsel unless they agree to this rule. You can emphasize this by saying, "There may be only one place on earth where you will not fight with each other this way, but it will be here. I expect Christians to act in ways that please God. So, what do you say?"

Contentious people will, of course, argue with you too. You must be ready to handle their disagreements, harsh words, angry looks, and/or insults. While you may begin to feel defensive or even riled at these things, you must learn to take them in stride, handling them in a manner that never allows them without comment, but never gets you upset. You must be strong, warding off these attacks, remembering that you are simply the latest object to assault. You don't allow them to get under your skin, but neither do you allow them to go by unnoticed. Emphasize that "you are talking to one another in a hostile way. Remember, we agreed you would talk to me instead. Now, please go on with what you were about to say, only say it to me."

How do you help such people? You probably will find that a conference table will be useful (see the *Manual* for full information about this). Concisely stated this is an agreement to meet and discuss matters (allowing nothing but conferring with no hostility). One agrees to open the conference with prayer, the other is the secretary who takes progress notes to bring to counseling. All matters that cannot be settled between them are to be written down and brought to counseling where we will continue the session with the counselor helping out. If either one perceives that they have stopped conferring and are doing anything else, the other silently stands until the other says something like, "OK. Let's go on conferring." There is to be no argument about whether or not anyone should stand on any given occasion.

The Scriptures are to dominate everyone's thoughts throughout. After the initial prayer, one of the conferees reads a portion of Proverbs, beginning with chapter ten (at each conference, the next chapter should be read). The counselees should take an agreed upon number of conference sessions (no more than two per week), along with the time and place. That will keep down arguments about these things.

That is what to do with a couple who are contentious. But what about an individual who can't get along with other people? He probably won't admit to the true reason why people avoid him, but as you listen to him, and the accounts of what is happening in his life in relationship to others, you will quickly understand that his problem is contentiousness. When you are sure about this problem, tell him in no uncertain words that you think he has problems with others because of his contentiousness. He may or may not like it, but if you can prove from quotations that you have been taking down on your Weekly Record Form (see the *Manual* for more on this) for a couple of sessions, you can make the case.

To help him, you will give him assignments that will enable him to deal with others in a different manner. You can actually role play confrontations with his friend, his boss, his girl friend, and so forth. You can switch roles at times demonstrating how a Christian ought to talk to others. Then let him practice it. Now, you must stress that all of this training is done, not as an outward show, but as a way to accomplish what he has agreed he ought to do before the Lord. He has probably had to do some confessing of sin to some people, and he surely must understand that he is trying to change first of all to please God, not to win friends and influence people. In other words, all that he does must come from his heart. The same, of course, would be true of the couple who are beginning to use the conference table.

There are patterns, again, that are habitual ways of sinning. They must not only be broken, but (as I said elsewhere in this book) must be replaced with their biblical alternatives. You will explain the put off/put on dynamic found in Ephesians 4 and Colossians 3, and you will also emphasize radical amputation of the former ways that must be abandoned. In all of this, as in most counseling, there will be failures. Note these, how things ought to have gone instead of how they did, and encourage them to do better the next time. Don't allow them to become discouraged by failures. Simply have them acknowledge their failures, repent of them, and go on to do things the right way in the future.

Contentious persons are difficult to counsel because their argumentative spirit is constantly interrupting progress. But you must move ahead anyway, consistently telling them things like, "You did it again, now let's try it once more as a Christian should." Don't give up and if they want to honor God they will finally get the hang of it. Patience – in abundance – is what you will need.

Conniving

Not everyone coming for counsel really wants your help. That is to say, he may not want the help that you are anxious to offer. He may, instead, have an agenda that is contrary to Scripture that, with your assistance, he wants to actuate. What am I talking about? To understand, consider the following synopsis.

Roger has been dating one of the members of your congregation. He wants to marry her, but she has said that unless he professes faith in Christ, no marriage will take place. She comes to you with this question: "Should I keep seeing Roger?" You answer, of course (as the Bible directs), "No, Susan, you shouldn't lead him on thinking that he has a chance when he doesn't, since he isn't a believer." She breaks off with Roger. But she does continue to see him for a time to present the way of salvation to him. A couple of weeks later, Roger and Susan ask for an appointment. When they come it is plain from their opening statements that the object of their coming is to receive your blessing on a forthcoming marriage that Roger wants (Susan does too). Susan says, "Roger has become a Christian, and so is it OK for us to get married now?" Roger affirms this statement: "Yes, Susan told me all about becoming Christian, and now that I've become one I want to join your church."

Being of the suspicious mind, you wonder about this development so soon after speaking to Susan as you did. So, you begin to examine Roger's profession a bit.

I'm so glad to hear it whenever a person becomes a Christian. Tell me about your decision. I'd like very much to hear about it.

Roger stammers a little, then says, "Well, you see it's like this: Susan refused to marry me unless I became a Christian, so I thought about it and told her I would."

Sounds suspicious. So, you continue, "Did Susan tell you that you must repent of your sins, or did you come to that realization yourself?"

— Uh… Well, sorta' both things happened.

— She told you and you figured it applied to you?

— That's about it.

— So, recognizing and confessing that you were a sinner against God, what did you do next?

— I became a Christian.

— Yes, Roger, but how did that happen?

— I told you – Susan told me I had to become a Christian, and so I did.

— I understand that is what you said, but what I'm getting at is that when you confessed your sin to God, what did you do next?

— Well, as I said, I decided to become a Christian.

— I told him about how Jesus died for our sins, Pastor (Susan adds).

— Good, Susan. What did you do about that fact Roger?

— I'm not sure what you mean.

— Did you place your trust in Christ as your Savior.

— I guess so.

And so it goes. Roger has no clue as to what salvation is. You, then, explain the Gospel and call upon him to believe it, but you make it clear that if he claims to believe, it must be "for real," and that it will take some time for him to prove that his faith is genuine before you can recommend that he and Susan marry. Roger gets a bit huffy about that and says that he sees no difficulty in the way since he has "become a Christian." You speak later, privately, with Susan and warn her about Roger's less than credible profession of faith. He has already told her that he wasn't going to get into the "rigmarole" that you "handed out to him." Susan's eyes are opened.

It will not be the only time that you will participate in such a conversation. There are a number of Rogers in this world – and Susans as well. Be prepared for them to tell you anything that they think you will approve of in order to use you as a crowbar to get leverage on another person!

Surely, you get the point: whether it is someone wanting to convince you that he/she should be married by assenting to whatever you suggest is necessary, or whether it is a person wanting to become a member of your church, it turns out, in order to sell a dietary supplement plan to your members. You will encounter them all. If your parsonage is located next to the church, you will get your share of people knocking on the door with "convincing" stories about how they need money. You will, naturally, send them to one of your deacons who has been trained to distinguish those with real needs from the connivers who want a few bucks in order to get a couple of drinks. And, where you find that a Roger is confused, but genuine, and that the needy person is telling you the truth, you and the church will help them – always in a proper fashion. Having been stung once, as I and many other well-meaning pastors have, if you allow it to happen again, you should think twice about your vulnerability. Such persons not only hurt others, they also hurt themselves.

What do you do with Rogers, Susans, sellers of diet plans and drunks? You don't simply dismiss them when you discover that they are insincere, you attempt to give them the real help that they need. You talk to them about what they are up to, how serious it is to attempt to "use" God to attain some unworthy purpose, how God looks unfavorably upon a false profession of belief in Christ, and so on. And, through confronting about the sin of conniving to get their way through falsehood, you try to bring them to true repentance and faith in Christ.

Confused

Many of the people that we have talked about thus far, in addition to their other peculiarities are, as a complicating problem, somewhat confused. But there are also those whose principal problem is confusion. It is the latter about which I wish to write in this chapter. Confusion is not unusual in counseling. Most counselees, at least in the beginning, exhibit a degree of confusion. They are in a new context, wondering how things will come out, what will take place, what their responsibilities are, and so forth. It is not that sort of confusion, unless it continues for an unduly long time (or increases) that concerns us. It will dissipate. Instead, we must think for a while about people who in their entire demeanor exhibit confusion.

The first thing to consider is drugs. Many mind-altering drugs can lead to confusion. Some are illicit drugs, others are prescription drugs. Few OTC drugs can do so, but some, mishandled, may have that effect upon some people. The PDI screens for various drugs of that sort. Moreover, it helps detect whether or not there are perceptual problems that a person is having from medication. See *The Christian Counselor's Manual* for information about how to determine from the PDI what, if any, drugs may be affecting your counselee. Bob Smith's *The Christian Counselor's Medical Desk Reference* will also assist you in discovering what drugs have what effect upon people, and how to deal with those who are affected by them. Since these other more definitive works are available, we shall not deal with confusion resulting from drugs in this chapter.

Among other things, there are people who are confused about counseling, about doctrine, about how to interpret and use Scripture, and about their place in counseling itself. Whenever you detect an inordinate amount of confusion, or confusion that is not cleared up by itself as counseling proceeds, it is well to stop whatever it is that you are doing to spend time discovering what is the source of the confusion. In most instances, you will want to address the problem directly: "Sandy, you seem uncertain or, perhaps, confused about what I have been saying. Can you tell me what it is that is unclear?" Perhaps you might receive an answer something like this: "Pastor, I can't quite understand what you're up to. You're telling me to do this homework assignment, but that isn't the way I've been taught about how to deal with life difficulties."

"What have you been taught to change your sinful behavior?"

"To yield, to let go, and let God. If I try to *do* something myself, then that would be attempting to change by means of the arm of the flesh."

Obviously, if you were to receive that sort of answer (or any answer that revealed a misunderstanding of the Bible that would hinder counseling) you would immediately need to stop and handle the doctrinal problem. Otherwise, you'd get nowhere with the homework you were intending to give.[1] So, doctrinal confusion that stands in the way of counseling must be cleared up or more than likely counseling will fail. I say doctrinal confusion that hinders counseling because it is impossible to deal with all doctrinal issues in counseling. The regular ministry of the Word will, over time, do so as God uses and blesses it.

Other problems leading to confusion may exist. Someone may be confused about why he is present. Husbands, and children dragged to counseling by parents, often give evidence of such confusion. "I don't know what my wife hopes to do by

---

1. You can find detailed information about Keswick theology and its errors in the *Manual*. Here, it must suffice to mention that the Scriptures require us to "do" things (you can point this out from many passages) and not expect God to do them for us, instead of us. But it is also important to note that we must do them not in our own strength (as though we were capable of pleasing God by our efforts alone) but by the power of the Holy Spirit, working through the Word of God ministered and followed in faith.

insisting that I accompany her. The problem is hers, not mine." Or, possibly, you may hear a teenager saying, "Look, this counseling stuff isn't for me. I get along just fine with my peers. My old man is the only one I don't get along with." Now, in these cases, you may discover that the counselees are not really confused about their role, but are simply affecting confusion as an excuse for their desire to get out of it. On the other hand, they may genuinely be confused. In the former situation, you must work with all involved to convince (if possible) that counseling is necessary, if for no other reason, than to settle differences between the parties involved. Obviously the husband and wife disagree on a vital issue – which is the cause of the marital difficulty. In the case of the teen, a similar issue must be dealt with. In the latter case, where there is genuine confusion, that must be clarified before counseling may successfully be pursued. "Tell me, Sally, why do you think it is necessary for Phil to come with you." And, from the answer that you receive, counseling can take off in whatever direction it should. The teen obviously thinks that there is a problem only with his father. Ask him what the problem is. Get his parents' views as well. Then you will know what the problem is and what to do to successfully solve it. If the wife agrees with the son, then you have a problem with her and her husband to handle, not merely with the father and the son. It may be that she and her boy have ganged up against the father, the mother hindering his discipline by doing so. Other possible scenarios may develop from your questioning, but such pursuit of what is really going on, so as to clear up any confusion that exists, is essential. In other words, confusion on anyone's part is detrimental to counseling. Jesus had to clear up the confusion from the mind a man steeped in the Scriptures, but who did not understand their import, in order to help him. Certainly you know the story of Nicodemus (John 3), but did you notice how Jesus told him that He expected more from him as "a ruler of the Jews?" Nicodemus ought to have understood that the Spirit brings newness of life from the plain reference to the fact in Ezekiel 36:26, 27:

> I will give you a new heart and put a new spirit within you; I will remove your heart of stone and give you a heart of flesh. I will place My Spirit within you and cause you to follow My statutes and carefully observe My ordinances (HCSB, see also Ezekiel 18:31).[1]

Confusion of the sort we have been examining can stem from any number of sources, as I have noted. But the important thing to remember is that apart from removing it, confusion will usually be a hindrance to successful counseling.

---

1. Incidentally, notice that, in reference to the Keswick theology previously referenced, the Spirit "causes" the believer to "observe": God's commands.

Silent

They just won't talk. I say "won't" because they can. If they only would. I'm not describing people who have speech disabilities, but those who, instead of answering or communicating when it is appropriate to do so, keep silent. It is irritating in counseling, and indeed must be elsewhere, to try to carry on a conversation with such persons. They will give you meaningless nods, grunts, or looks instead of talk.

Speech is crucial to friendship, to functioning well, and to relationships of every sort. They call him "Silent Joe" down at work. He will discuss anything that he is asked to talk about with his superiors, but he virtually cuts off communication with everyone else. And when he does talk, it is to the point, crisp and concise. He doesn't waste words. There is never any chit-chat, no friendly comments, no indication that he even notices others unless they make the effort to get a reply from him. He's a good worker – that's why they don't fire him. But as a human being at shop, he's a cipher.

There are reasons why people don't carry on normal conversations with others. There is no need to examine them since they vary widely. What is important is to deal with your counselee's speechlessness. Others have finally decided to put up with it no longer, so they have dragged, bludgeoned, or otherwise coerced him into coming for counseling. He obviously doesn't want to be here. He may say nothing, if he's that resistant. You can ask him how he sees things, but you won't receive an answer. If he says, "Oh, I don't know," you did well to get that out of him. So, you are going to have problems.

What you will finally end up doing, if nothing else works, is having a very confrontational talk with him (or, I should say *to* him). It may be a lecture, but it's one that he needs to hear.

You call yourself a Christian. OK. Then you are going to learn how to live like one. And that includes talking. Not only ought Christians to talk to God, but to one another as well. There is a verse in Ephesians 4 that is determinative in this matter: "EACH ONE MUST SPEAK TRUTH WITH HIS NEIGHBOR, since we are members of one another" (Ephesians 4:25). If you don't understand that verse, I'll make it clear to you. Paul was talking about lying and told the Ephesians to put it "off." Then, he wrote what I have just read to you. He was saying that because Christians are united to Christ, they are also united to one another. And, as persons who must live, work, and fellowship with one another in the church and in the home, they must communicate the truth because all parts need to understand what the other parts are thinking if they are to coordinate their efforts. And, guess what? They must do so by speech! Now, as the part of the human body must function together in order to accomplish anything, they must not work at odds with each other. They must all know what to do about any action that involves them. One hand cannot reach out to take up the spoon to eat while the other hand is trying to hold it back. Their purposes must be identical if they are to accomplish anything. The same is true with individuals. Your silence, rather than communication that helps coordinate what you do in relationship to others, is creating just as much havoc as if the parts of your anatomy were each serving his own purpose regardless of the other. You'd probably never even get the spoon to your mouth. How do you expect others to relate to you when you won't give them a clue to what is going on inside of you? You must learn to speak the truth in love, recognizing that you are not a lone wolf, but a member of the same body as other believers. Now that I've lectured you, what do you have to say?

His response, if any, will be interesting and will give you the clues as to what to do next. If he continues to give you the silent treatment, then dismiss the session with words similar to these: "OK. You claim to be converted. If you are, you can see from the verse that I just quoted, that you are sinning by silence. There is a time to be silent, certainly. But you are silent when you ought to speak. If you have difficulty talking I will help you. If you persist in this I cannot. The matter may even reach the level of church discipline if you continue your silence and fail to receive help. I want you to go home this week and think and pray about what I just said. And, then, next week I will expect to see you and *hear* what you have to say. Now, let's pray." [He is dismissed.]

Short? Yes. But that's because I did all the talking. The counselee needs to think about that verse and the ways in which he is violating God's command. So, let him do so. He'll have plenty of time to do it since he probably won't be having conversations around the water cooler.

Intellectual

To be smart is good. To be educated is fine. To be wise is better than both. But to be an "intellectual"? Now that's another matter. I suppose that people vary as to their definition of an intellectual, and may not countenance what I am about to say because of that. But to me, an intellectual is someone whose education is showing. That is to say, he doesn't keep it to himself, but in one way or another allows it to protrude. There is something stuffy about him. He rises above the crowd, not to lead them but, to look down on them. He is haughty about his education and he knows that he has more than many others. Yet, the farmer out on his tractor in the field knows more about mechanics, plowing, sowing, reaping, and agriculture in general than most of us. But, ordinarily, he isn't looked upon as an intellectual! Why not? He excels in what he is doing, he can fix things, bring in the food that the intellectual eats, and so forth. The intellectual knows something about something too. But he's looked up to rather than the highly knowledgeable farmer. The reason for this is simple. He can talk a good game.

The intellectual is principally a talker. Few people would be called intellectual if they did not parade it with speech. The normal person adjusts his speech habits to the group with which he is associating. He isn't out of place. The intellectual is always out of place if he can help it. His education is flaunted by his speech. He uses terms and words that have to do with his area of expertise, and caries them over into everyday conversations. He has one manner of speaking, he cannot (or won't) adjust. He is hard to be around for very long since he is everlastingly speaking in highfalutin ways. It is not smart, it is not wise to do so, but he does. Why? Because he is an intellectual. He is in a class by himself (although, at times other intellectuals match wits with him).

What people need to learn is wisdom. Education without wisdom; natural "smarts" without wisdom is barren, unhelpful, and sometimes offensive. Indeed, when education, or the fruits of it are displayed by the intellectual, he can cause others who may or may not be every bit as smart and as fully educated as he, to turn the other way. Then when he comes into counseling because he is having problems with interpersonal relationships of one sort or another, he will talk like an academic about his problems. There will be no warmth – either of anger or of love, in his speech. He will sound like the words of a government issued pamphlet. He will try to snow you with his speech. That's precisely when I begin to talk to him in the sort of language that I am using in this article. He doesn't like it, perhaps, but if he wants help he is forced to listen to the *koine*[1] that I spout forth. Paul was a highly educated and intelligent man. But he was also wise. And it is interesting that he wrote to his churches and fellow workers, not in the language of the second sophistic that was popular among the intellectuals of his day, but in the common street language that everyone knew. His education didn't hang out, but it cannot be missed by anyone who has spent time exegeting his remarkable letters.

All that Paul was is what an intellectual isn't. All that Luke, who was a skilled and learned physician was, the intellectual isn't. He and Paul could write with skill, but never in a way that the farmer with his horse and plow could not understand. It was the scholasticism of the Middle Ages that took the common language away from the people as a whole. Scholastics today might do the same if they thought that the situation warranted it. The sophist charmed people with his rhetoric and his speech tactics. But even Socrates, who was no intellectual but knew all of their ploys, refused to use them to save his own skin when he was brought before the court at Athens. He drank the hemlock rather than employ sophistry.

---

1. The "common" (as the word means) market language of the Hellenistic period. New Testament Greek is written in *koine* Greek.

Today, there is something akin to that in the intellectual who so protrudes his education that he hits you in the face with it. The intellectual is impressed by his education, not his intellect. He is a devotee of intellectual*ism*.

When you encounter him in counseling he may try to snow you with his language and a few facts that are part of his "intellectual" arsenal. But don't be put off by him. Speak wisdom in the *koine*. That may bring him down to earth. Make it clear to him that you don't need to let your knowledge and training show; you just use it. You are comfortable with your language because the common man is also comfortable with it. Talk turkey to him about how he puts people off with his high-hatted speech, how he insulates himself from others by the wall of manifested education he exudes. Bring him down to earth. Tell him to learn a vocabulary that communicates, just as the New Testament vocabulary did. He may need to repent of pride if that is the cause of his poor communicative skills. But, on the other hand, he may not. He may simply have fallen into the patterns of speech that he uses from association with other scholastics. Academia should not be brought over into real life, and he needs to understand that.

Conclusion

This book has been written, as you understand (now that you have read it), to help you identify and assist people with attitudes and habits that complicate counseling. Many of the traits considered have not been dealt with in other books. Some of them are peculiar to a few individuals, most to many. The kinds of traits identified, however, are of a character that, if you are not alert to them, you may bypass in counseling. When that happens, the result is that counseling may bog down. Because a counselor has not been aware that they might be present, he is likely to wonder what has gone wrong. Giving attention to the matters that I have set forth, therefore, will obviate that unfortunate result.

Probably, since your mind has been occupied in studying these somewhat unusual factors that some people exhibit, you will tend to think of other characteristics that I have not singled out. Clearly, the list could be lengthened significantly. Besides, it is not necessary to mention many more than I have since you are now in a mode of thinking outside of the box. You, yourself, will (I hope) be on the lookout for these and others.

I trust that this study will be a beginning that you will continue to pursue on your own. May the Lord bless your counseling richly and help you in the project of discovering other traits as well. Blessings!

Appendix

The following forms may be copied and used. Copy each page at 150% and it will fit on a standard 8.5" x 11" piece of paper.

Personal Data Inventory
_____ Church Counseling Ministry

IDENTIFICATION DATA:

Name: _____ Phone: _____

Address: _____

Occupation: _____ Business Phone: _____

Sex:___ Birth Date:_____ Age: _____ Separated:_____ Divorced: ___ Widowed:_____

Education: (Last year completed) _____ Other training: _____

Referred here by: _____Address: _____

HEALTH INFORMATION:

Rate Your Health: Very Good: _____ Good: _____ Average: ___ Declining:_____ Other: _____

Your approximate weight: _____lbs.; Recent weight changes: Lost_____ lbs. Gained _____lbs.

List all important, present or past, injuries, illnesses or handicaps:_____

Date of Last Medical Examination: _____ Report: _____

Your Physician:_____ Address: _____

Are you currently taking medication? Yes __ No ___ If so, what? _____

Have you used drugs for other than medical purposes? Yes ___ No ___ Which Drugs?_____

Have you ever had a severe emotional upset? Yes _____ No_____ Explain:_____

Have you ever been arrested? Yes _____ No_____ Explain: _____

Are you willing to sign a release of information form so that your counselor may write for social, psychiatric, or medical reports? Yes _____ No _____

RELIGIOUS BACKGROUND:

Denominational preference: _____ Church: _____ Member: _____

Church Attendance per month (circle): 0 1 2 3 4 5 6 7 8 9 10+

Church Attended in childhood: _____ Were you baptized? Yes __ No ____

Religious background of spouse (if married): _____

Do you consider yourself a religious person? Yes ___ No ____ Uncertain _____

Do you believe in God? Yes ___ No ____ Uncertain _____

Do you pray to God? Never _____ Occasionally_____ Often _____

Are you saved? Yes _____ No_____ Not sure what you mean _____

How much do you read the Bible? Never_____ Occasionally _____ Often _____

Do you have regular family devotions? Yes_____ No _____

Explain recent changes in your religious life, if any:_____

PERSONALITY INFORMATION

Have you ever had any psychotherapy or counseling before? Yes_____ No _____

If yes, list counselor or therapist and dates: _____

PERSONALITY INFORMATION (CONTINUED):

What was the outcome? _____

_____

CIRCLE ANY OF THE FOLLOWING WORDS WHICH BEST DESCRIBE YOU NOW: active ambitious self-confident persistent nervous hard-working impatient impulsive moody often-blue excitable imaginative calm serious easy-going shy good-natured introvert extrovert likeable leader quiet hard-boiled submissive self-conscious lonely sensitive
other: _____

Have you ever thought people were watching you? Yes___   No ____
Do people's faces ever seem distorted?   Yes___   No ____
Do you ever have difficulty distinguishing faces?   Yes___   No ____
Do colors ever seem too bright?   Yes___   No ____   Too Dull? Yes ____   No _____
Are you sometimes unable to judge distance?   Yes___   No ____
Have you ever had hallucinations?   Yes___   No ____
Are you afraid of being in a car?   Yes___   No ____
Is your hearing exceptionally good?   Yes___   No ____
Do you have problems sleeping?   Yes___   No ____

MARRIAGE AND FAMILY INFORMATION:

Name of spouse:_____   Address: _____
Phone: _____   Occupation:_____   Business Phone: _____
Spouse's Age: _____   Education (yrs.):_____   Religion: _____
Is spouse willing to come for counseling? Yes _____   No _____   Uncertain _____
Have you ever been separated? Yes _____   No ___   When? from _____   to _____
Have either of you ever filed for divorce? Yes_____   No _____   When?_____
Date of marriage: _____   Ages when married: Husband_____   Wife _____
How long did you know your spouse before marriage? _____
Length of steady dating with spouse: _____   Length of engagement: _____
Give brief information about any previous marriages: _____

INFORMATION ABOUT CHILDREN:

PM*	Name	Age	Sex	Living Y/N	Education in years	Marital Status	Living w/ you? Y/N

* Check column if child is by previous marriage of either spouse.
If you were reared by anyone other than your own parents, briefly explain: _____

How many older brothers_____   sisters _____   do you have?
How many younger brothers _____   sisters _____   do you have?

1. What is the main problem as you see it (What brings you here)? _____

_____

_____

_____

_____

_____

_____

_____

_____

_____

_____

2. What have you done about it? _____

_____

_____

_____

_____

_____

_____

_____

_____

_____

_____

3. What do you want us to do about it? _____

_____

_____

_____

_____

_____

_____

_____

_____

_____

_____

4. What further information about yourself should we know?_____

_____

_____

_____

_____

_____

_____

_____

_____

_____